5/11/99

COOKIN'
WITH THE
CLEAVERS

To
Jennifer!
Thank for the GiG!

Lee Bada - Bing Bada - Boom!

Steve

COOKIN' WITH THE CLEAVERS

The Clever Cleaver Brothers

Stephen J. Cassarino
and
Lee N. Gerovitz

WYNWOOD ® Press
New York, New York

Photos taken on the set of "Live With Regis and Kathie Lee" are used with permission and courtesy of "Live With Regis and Kathie Lee"/WABC-TV.

Interior illustrations by Maureen Ruckdeschel.

Front cover and centerfold photos by Larry W. Scott; lighting director Bill Holshevnikoff.

Library of Congress Cataloging-in-Publication Data

Cassarino, Stephen J.
    Cookin' with the Cleavers / Stephen J. Cassarino and Lee N.
Gerovitz.
        p.   cm.
    Includes index.
    ISBN 0-922066-47-7 : $12.95
    1. Cookery. 2. Cookin' with the Cleavers (Television program)
I. Gerovitz, Lee N.   II. Title.
TX714.C376   1990
64.15–dc20   90-12476
                                                           CIP

Published by WYNWOOD™ Press
New York, New York
Printed in the United States of America

DEDICATION

The dedication of a book usually goes to family members. We're not sure exactly why this happens, except that it is usually family, be it a spouse and children or parents and siblings, that stand beside an author during the rough years on the way to success.

Although "The Clever Cleaver Brothers" have never been ones to follow trends or tradition, we, also, want to dedicate this book with warmth and love to our families.

Growing up in East Hartford, Connecticut, and being the oldest Cassarino child, my mom and dad always gave me the room to experiment and grow. They showed me their trust and confidence in my ability to use good judgment in whatever I wanted to do. So, Mom and Dad, this is just my small way of saying thanks for letting me run off to different parts of the globe to gain my "worldly" experience and for encouraging me to go to college and make the most of my life.

Eric, Maria, and baby Jaclyn, and my other sister, Lydia, and my brother, Dave – thanks for being true fans and friends. Over the years that I've been in California and in business, your frequent cards and telephone calls have been the secret ingredient in a terrific recipe. Your support has always been there when I needed it.

And, Mamma Gerovitz, how do I say thank you for everything you did for me while I was growing up? The things you did and the sacrifices you made went way beyond the call of being a mother. You instilled in all us kids a sense of honesty, integrity, and a strong work ethic.

Growing up in a small town like Waterford, Connecticut, it would have been easy to go to school, get a job, and never leave town. But, from the time we were youngsters, you told all of us that we could be anything in this world that we wanted to be. You always had nothing but nice things to say about everyone with whom you came in contact, and you taught us to do everything in a worthwhile, productive, and positive manner.

The simple building blocks that you taught us, like always keeping our shoes shined, always carrying a clean, pressed handkerchief, and always offering a firm handshake, along with integrity, honesty, and living our dreams, was the perfect foundation to a prosperous future.

Along with my Mom, Jan Gerovitz, I dedicate this book to my sister Marlene, and her husband, Joe, and their children Robin, Janet, Joey, and Sherry; my sister Linda, and her husband, David, and Linda's son, Ricardo (Bubba); my sister Robin, and her son, Wayne Ellis; my multi-talented brother Jay, who has been so supportive out here in San Diego, doing everything from building props to shuttling us to the airport; my brother Jody, who is an excellent chef himself and a terrific brother; my brother Randy – a wild and crazy guy with whom I love to go on vacation; and my brother Todd, his wife, Liisa, and their son, Michael Todd. When I go back East, Todd and Liisa open their home to me and roll out the red carpet.

CONTENTS

An array of Clever Cleaver favorites that can be used as passed hors d'oeuvres or as a first course at the table.

Breakfast and brunch were never easier and more enjoyable than with "The Clever Cleaver Brothers." No yolkin'.

With a simple, basic bread recipe, let us show you how to make several varieties. Don't have your next pizza delivered – we'll show you how to make it.

Do you enjoy seafood and fish as much as we do? Good, try it our way.

No, not "The Clever Cleaver Brothers." From Stir-Fry Beef to Veal Marsala.

If you're ready to BBQ those ribs, bake your ham, or stuff your chops, this is the chapter for you. Those delicious pork dinners and more.

Yes, you too will enjoy Broiled Lamb Chops and Roast Leg of Lamb as never before.

onfn(ери

GO FLY THE COOP 125

Chicken, chicken, and more chicken, along with Roast Turkey and Roast Long Island Duckling. Each with all the trimmings.

LOTSA LINGUINE 139

Lotsa pasta. From Fettuccine Alfredo to Baked Lasagna, with a lot more in between.

EVERYONE'S GRAZING 155

Potatoes and vegetables to make any meal complete and every plate beautiful.

GONE BANANAS! 171

Yes, we're a little crazy, but this chapter is not describing us. Top a delicious evening with one of our simple and wonderful desserts.

EAT RIGHT, GET TIGHT 183

. . . and you'll be out of sight. No, these are not words to a new James Brown song. This chapter will help you shop for the best foods. Then, we'll show you a few simple changes you can make in the kitchen to make a more healthful meal.

FOOD, POTS and PANS, and KNOW-HOW 191

This chapter could also be called "Ingredients, Equipment, and Techniques." We help you to understand herbs and spices. Different types of knives will no longer be a mystery. The myriad of pots and pans will no longer be foreign. We'll give you the "know-how" so you can move in the kitchen as if you were gliding on the dance floor. Check out this chapter for a wealth of culinary information:

ACKNOWLEDGMENTS

While most authors thank individuals who have assisted in the writing of a book, "The Clever Cleaver Brothers" would like to take this opportunity to thank several people who have been very supportive during the entire time we have been in business. Their encouragement and support have been instrumental in propelling us to the point in our careers where a book would be appropriate.

How many people actually want to thank their accountant? Our accountants are a lot more than just dreaded tax preparers. Jim Bobryk was the very first person we went to when we had the idea to produce a video cookbook. He helped us organize our original partnership agreement and he referred us to individuals who helped us get the ball rolling. And Beverly Gibson Still, who still works with us today, organized our books so we could clearly see where our money was being spent. Bev is a lot more than an accountant; she was more like a big sister who worried more about the rocky road of a new business than we did. We still look forward to meeting with Bev each month to go over the books and talk about our new, upcoming events. And, yes Bev, no matter how big "The Clever Cleaver Brothers" become, we will never outgrow your services and friendship.

Along with accountants, attorneys are often considered overpaid, necessary evils. We're pleased to say that our attorney is different. People say that conducting business with friends can quite often end a good friendship. Our attorney is the exception to the rule. Andrew Kaplan, or "Kappy" as we refer to him, has been our friend a lot longer than he has been our attorney. He treats people with the same honesty, integrity, and sincerity with which he practices law. It is no wonder that he is such a terrific individual and successful attorney. In many ways that we are cognizant of, Kappy is responsible for our prospering, after the typical entrepreneurial start.

We would like to thank KTTY TV-69 for recognizing a good opportunity and working with us to get our "Cookin' With The Cleavers" television show on the airwaves.

And, when we got the green light for "Cookin' With The Cleavers," we needed a dynamic kitchen set. While most people balk at a challenge, Rick

Fahmie of Kitchen Expo of La Jolla rose to the occasion. Being young himself and having recently started his own business, he did not have a "9-to-5" attitude. Rick designed and built the best television kitchen that we have ever seen. And, as we continued to grow, Rick and Kitchen Expo were right there to assist us with our new challenges.

Tom and Kathie Steele are unique entrepreneurs themselves. They have the company that created and produced the CHEF salt and pepper shakers that we use on our shows, the Clever Cleaver refrigerator chalkboards, and a myriad of other products. More important, they have always been there to share lunch and a good laugh with us, and to boost our morale when needed.

When we produced "Cooking For Compliments" in 1984, we had no idea that the people who were retained to do the music would be such an important element in our shows down the road. Michael Hamilton, head of FAHBR Productions, refined our raps and created the music to make our shows sizzle. We are happy to have Michael as a friend and fortunate to have his talents available to us.

Bob Hanson, president of Angostura International Ltd., is a lot more than just a business associate. From the onset, Bob recognized our talents and looked for creative ways for us to work together. More than that, when we meet with Bob, Bill Chango, Jerome Bongiovanni, Tom Jacko, Evelyn Toner, and everyone at Angostura, it is more like being with family than business. We are glad to know all of you and pleased to have you as part of our success story.

Friends, true friends, are critical to success. We appreciate the friendship and support of Tom Piascik, Michael Bonanno, Jr., Dean Abrams, Eric Krueger, Mike and Sharon Hughes, Chuck Leal, Aly Kahn, and Lisa and Sammy Tomeo. Often, when we go to the East Coast on business, we sneak down to the South Jersey shore and share some rest and relaxation with Lisa and Sammy and a great meal at their Port O' Call restaurant.

And speaking of friends, we have a very special friend right here in San Diego. I (Lee) worked with Marc Robert Mann at Foodmaker, and we have all been very good friends ever since. Marc accompanies us to many of our television and video shoots, and he is always ready with some good-humored sarcasm. We look forward to the day when we can lure Marc away from his enterprises to be part of our business.

We are grateful to everyone at the "Live with Regis & Kathie Lee" show for giving us our national television debut and asking us back so many times.

Not only has the national exposure been excellent for our growth, but we always enjoy doing their show.

And, speaking of shows, we really enjoyed our several appearances on "L.A. in the Morning" with Stephanie Edwards. Not only is Stephanie a very warm and comfortable host, she has also become a special friend to us. We appreciate her always going the extra mile.

No East Coast trip is complete without an appearance on "The Fairfield Exchange" television show. Dave and Becky are fun and gracious hosts and we never get tired of seeing them. Now that we think about it, fortunately, they don't tire of us. Thanks also to Suzanne Smith for always being so accommodating.

We would like to express our appreciation to Herb Golden, Larry Scott, and the entire production crew at The Helmeka Group for working with us on various projects. Aside from being very professional, they are real nice people to work with.

Speaking of nice people with professional attitudes, we would like to acknowledge Cathie Johns and Joey Garcia from Creative Edge for their contribution to several of our projects. We write about 98 percent of our own material; I think they account for most of the other 2 percent.

This section would not be complete without mentioning our alma mater, Johnson & Wales University in Providence, Rhode Island. Not only did we meet and begin our routines while attending Johnson & Wales, we also received excellent culinary arts training. Thank you, Johnson & Wales, for the excellent education and for providing us with such a solid culinary foundation. Additionally, we appreciate your continued interest and support towards our venture.

Is acknowledging your publisher acceptable? For us, Wynwood Press took action at a time when other publishers were simply talking about doing a book with us. Richard Re saw us on "The Fairfield Exchange" television show in Connecticut and liked what he saw. Before we knew it, ba da bing – ba da boom, we were refining our manuscript. We really appreciate the excitement and enthusiasm expressed by everyone at Wynwood Press toward our project.

To Rod and E. J. at G&G Designs/Communications, thank you both for your advice and technical assistance with the photos in this book. We appreciate your never-ending patience with our never-ending questions. In the end, the proof is in the photos.

"The Clever Cleaver Brothers" send a very special acknowledgment to all our viewers and fans who have made us so popular. Your cards, letters, and telephone calls mean a lot to us. From the onset, you have given our unique, lighthearted style your seal of approval. You showed us all along that we were heading in the right direction.

Last, but certainly not least, "The Clever Cleaver Brothers" would like to thank each other for possessing and contributing the elements necessary for success. The factors required for any successful venture, no less an entrepreneurial start-up, are too numerous to mention. As a matter of fact, most of these elements could not be identified, even if we were to try.

INTRODUCTION

Lee and Steve were best friends in college. But, as amazing as it will sound, they spoke only once in three years after they both left Johnson & Wales University. While in England, Steve called Lee, who was in Thousand Oaks, California, at the time, to invite him to dinner. It seems Steve was cooking dinner for eight "birds" and needed help in balancing the table.

As fate would have it, Steve's first stop in the States was San Diego, not knowing that Lee was also in San Diego. The two ran into each other on Steve's very first day back. You should have heard them reminiscing; everyone else on the beach did!

OH! YOU WANT TO KNOW MORE. . . .

In late 1984, Lee and Steve started their business with the production of a 60-minute video cookbook, which was geared toward the beginner, called "Cooking For Compliments." The videotape employs a lighthearted approach to put the viewer at ease.

Because young adults feel so comfortable learning from "The Clever Cleaver Brothers," the video cookbook is being used as part of the curriculum in many high school home economics classes across the country.

After producing "Cooking For Compliments," the team appeared as guests on more than a dozen television and radio shows in San Diego and Los Angeles. They were also featured in several newspaper and magazine articles nationally.

In October 1986, they took San Diego by surprise with the premiere of their own half-hour, weekly cooking show called "Cookin' With The Cleavers." The show has a very unique format that is as entertaining as it is educational.

WHY THE SHOW?

GOOD QUESTION! Even during the time we produced our video cookbook, we saw a huge void on television that wasn't being filled by the available television chefs. We felt that their approach was far too serious, gearing their material toward chefs, not people.

When we put our show together, we vowed to be different. We became known as "The People Chefs" because we were intent on showing people how to cook and how to have lots of fun while doing it. We had no intention of showing chefs how to cook.

Not only would the menus be geared toward people, we would also use everyday equipment. With practicality being the name of the game, we didn't want to use the fancy, expensive pots and pans that most people did not have.

It was also important for us to explain the cooking procedure with step-by-step instructions. "The Clever Cleaver Brothers" did not want to baffle the viewers with big words and culinary terms that only our fellow culinary grads could understand.

We also saw that many cooking shows used fancy, expensive, and impractical ingredients that the viewers could never find at their local market. In keeping with the show's overall theme, we vowed to use only readily available ingredients. If we chose to use a specialty ingredient, we would always give a practical alternative that could be easily found. We even took it a step further. Every show included a 3-minute "market segment," where we took the viewer to the market, specialty shop, or another unique location. Using our fun approach, we shopped for our ingredients and provided interesting product information at the same time.

"Cookin' With The Cleavers" took off like a rocket. Viewer response was so positive that after we were on the air for just two months, KTTY moved us from the original 7:30 A.M. time slot to 11:00 every Saturday morning. We were awarded The Golden Halo Award by The Southern California Motion Picture Council of Hollywood for excellence in family and educational programming. Additionally, "The Clever Cleaver Brothers" were nominated for an EMMY Award by the San Diego chapter of The National Academy of Television Arts and Sciences, in the "performer" category.

Presently, we are in the process of producing our show for national television. At the same time, we continue to build our audience with regular appearances on the nationally syndicated "Live With Regis & Kathie Lee" show, as well as many regional shows across the country.

Our viewers feel very comfortable with us because it is obvious by watching us that we really do enjoy cooking and we always have a good time in the kitchen.

OK, WE BUY THE SHOW. BUT WHAT'S THE STORY WITH THE BOOK?

We thought you'd never ask. We already mentioned that we are "The People Chefs," so all our recipes have to be practical. Additionally, all our recipes have to pass The Clever Cleaver S.E.E. Test: they have to be *simple* for you, *easy* to prepare, and *elegant*, as you would expect.

"The Clever Cleaver Brothers" create and test all the recipes so we know they really work. As further testimony, we have received many calls and letters from viewers stating how pleased they were with our recipes. Viewers were so taken by the simplicity and elegance of our menus, we continually received requests to write a cookbook.

As a side benefit, we also wanted to create a unique alternative for everyone who has suffered from the bar syndrome at one time or another. Remember hearing, "Do you come here often?" or how about, "What's your sign?" We wanted to offer a practical way to entertain someone you may want to impress. OK, even if you are not out to impress someone, you will still score some points with these recipes.

Many of the recipes in this book call for fresh herbs. "The Clever Cleaver Brothers" take advantage of their year-round availability in California. If this is not the case in your area, feel free to use dehydrated herbs. Taste your food as it is being prepared and adjust the flavor intensity of your seasonings as necessary.

Additionally, many of our recipes call for low-sodium soy sauce or very low-sodium Worcestershire sauce. Although we do not make a practice of recommending brands by name, we feel that it is necessary in this case.

Technically, any soy sauce or Worcestershire sauce will work in the recipes that call for them. However, why not enjoy the flavor and leave the salt behind? Many brands claim to be "lite," "mild," or "low-sodium," but we have found the ANGOSTURA low-sodium soy sauce and the ANGOSTURA low-sodium Worcestershire sauce to be the only true low-sodium products on the market. Taste the flavor, not the salt.

Many of our recipies call for bitters as an ingredient. Although at first this ingredient may sound foreign, we have probably all used or seen it.

Bitters has been around for more than 165 years. The only brand that we are aware of is ANGOSTURA. Just about every bar in the country has this small paper-wrapped bottle as a staple ingredient. It was most widely used as an ingredient in champagne cocktails, old-fashioneds, and manhattans.

With an aroma closely resembling that of cloves, this secret blend of herbs and spices enhances the flavor of many recipes. Give it a try. Most supermarkets stock bitters with the liquor supplies/mixes.

These recipes are going to fill your social void. Trust us, they work!

RECIPE FOR SUCCESS

From the secret archives hidden somewhere in Mission Beach, California, comes the ancient recipe used to create two gallant gladiators of the kitchen.

1. Commandeer 50 square feet of beach and slowly add 2 bargain sand chairs. Add to each chair an abundance wit and charm, and slowly incorporate 3 heaping handfuls of talent.
2. Without letting this come to a boil, carefully add lots of charisma, good looks, and about 5 pounds of nerve.
3. Fill to the brim with a concoction of stale jokes and tired routines, a full social calendar, and 1 clove of 20/20 vision.
4. Season generously with good taste, and coat liberally with 100% pure olive oil.
5. Place in direct sunlight for about 30 years, turning periodically.

You've just created the hottest thing to come along since the electric hair dryer.

THE CLEVER CLEAVER BROTHERS!

Anyone for an hors d'oeuvre?

LET'S GET STARTED

ASSORTED FRUIT IN ORANGE CROWN

2 large oranges

½ small honeydew melon

½ small cantaloupe melon

Small grapes as needed

1. Plane one end of orange to make a flat surface.
2. Cut top of orange in a zigzag pattern to make a crown.
3. Hollow out inside of orange.
4. Dice melons or scoop with small parisienne scoop.
5. Fill oranges with cut fruit and grapes.
6. Hold in refrigerator for use.

Too cool for comfort.

STEVE'S ITALIAN EGG ROLLS
16 egg rolls

8 ounces hot Italian sausage
1/3 cup frozen chopped spinach,
   defrosted
2 cloves garlic, minced
Few dashes bitters

1/4 cup grated Parmesan cheese
1 package large egg roll wrappers
Oil for frying
Sauce of choice

1. In sauté pan, crumble and brown sausage meat. Drain fat and cool meat.
2. Squeeze all liquid out of defrosted, chopped spinach and combine in mixing bowl with cooled sausage, garlic, bitters, and Parmesan cheese.
3. Cut large egg roll wrappers in half to yield pieces approximately 3 inches × 6 inches.
4. Place 1 level tablespoon of the mixture on the end of the wrapper nearest to you. Do not go all the way to the end of the wrapper with filling.
5. Moisten top of wrapper and halfway down sides of wrapper with water on fingertip.
6. Roll wrapper with mixture halfway up wrapper. Seal sides of wrapper by pressing down with palm of hand.
7. Fold in sides. Remoisten with water on fingertip and continue to roll.
8. Cover egg rolls tightly in plastic wrap and then in aluminum foil. Put in freezer. Egg rolls should not touch or they will freeze together.
9. Remove from freezer 30 minutes prior to use, to temper.
10. Fry egg rolls in 350-degree oil until golden brown.
11. Place on paper towels to drain. Serve warm with your favorite sauce. *CAUTION:* INSIDE FILLING IS VERY HOT!

CURRIED CHICKEN HORS D'OEUVRES
6–8 portions

½ chicken
18-ounce jar orange
* marmalade*
½ cup shredded coconut

½ cup sliced almonds
1 tablespoon curry powder
Croutons or crackers, as needed

1. Place the half chicken in water. Bring to a boil and turn to simmer. Cook for approximately 45 minutes, or until done.
2. Remove chicken from water and cool. Remove the skin and bones and dice chicken into ¼-inch pieces.
   NOTE: This chicken procedure should be done in advance. Store cut chicken in refrigerator for use.
3. In a sauté pan over medium heat, heat orange marmalade. Add diced chicken meat, coconut, almonds, and curry powder. Combine.
4. Continue to heat until most of the liquid is removed but do not let dry out.
5. Serve curried chicken on croutons or your favorite crackers.

Would you let these mugs date your daughter?

CHICKEN IN BRANDY SAUCE
2–3 portions

1 chicken, cooked and
   cooled
½ cup mayonnaise
1½ tablespoons ketchup

2 tablespoons brandy
¼ teaspoon garlic powder
Couple dashes bitters
¼ teaspoon white pepper

1. Finely dice the cooked and cooled chicken meat and hold for use.
2. In a bowl, mix the mayonnaise, ketchup, brandy, garlic powder, bitters, and white pepper.
3. Combine the diced chicken with the brandy sauce and hold in the refrigerator for use.

Serve the Chicken in Brandy Sauce in any of the following ways:
- Serve alongside a scoop of low-fat cottage cheese on a bed of mixed greens.
- Serve over your favorite chilled pasta salad recipe.
- Serve inside a sandwich.

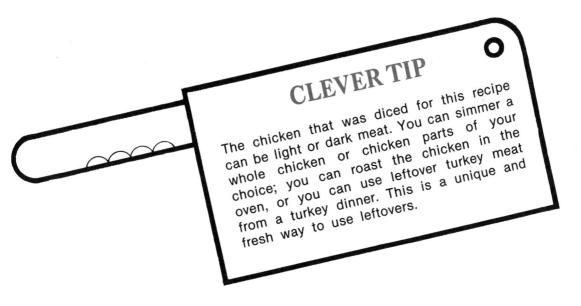

CLEVER TIP

The chicken that was diced for this recipe can be light or dark meat. You can simmer a whole chicken or chicken parts of your choice; you can roast the chicken in the oven, or you can use leftover turkey meat from a turkey dinner. This is a unique and fresh way to use leftovers.

MARINATED MEDLEY OF VEGETABLES WITH SHRIMP
2 portions

VINAIGRETTE DRESSING

1 cup salad oil
½ cup olive oil
½ cup red wine vinegar
1 clove garlic, minced
⅛ teaspoon white pepper
Pinch of salt

1 tablespoon chopped fresh basil
1 teaspoon chopped fresh oregano
1 teaspoon chopped fresh tarragon
⅛ teaspoon low-sodium Worcester-
  shire sauce
Few drops Tabasco sauce

1. Mix all ingredients in a mixing bowl at least 1 hour prior to use to obtain maximum flavor.
2. Store covered in the refrigerator until ready to use.

SHRIMP

12 medium shrimp   *½ lemon*

1. Peel shrimp, leaving the tail intact.
2. Using a small, sharp knife, cut a small incision along the back contour of the shrimp. Rinse under cold water to devein.
3. Add the juice of half a lemon to 6 cups water and bring to a boil.
4. Add cleaned shrimp and cook just until shrimp turn pink (approximately 4 minutes). DO NOT OVERCOOK.
5. Rinse shrimp under cold, running water to stop cooking. Store in refrigerator for service.

VEGETABLE MEDLEY

Rust leaf lettuce
Bibb lettuce
Cauliflower florets
Broccoli florets
Sliced zucchini squash

Sliced yellow squash
Carrot slices
Button mushrooms
Black pitted olives
1 red pepper

1. Rinse rust and bibb lettuce leaves. Pat dry with paper towels and refrigerate for service.
2. Bring salted water to a soft boil and blanch, one at a time, cauliflower florets, broccoli florets, sliced zucchini, and sliced yellow squash for 1 minute each. Remove each series of vegetables from water with a strainer and rinse under cold, running water to stop the cooking process. Refrigerate blanched vegetables until ready to use.
3. Rinse the button mushrooms and black olives under cold water but do not blanch. Refrigerate until ready to use.
4. Approximately 1 hour prior to service, toss the vegetables (not the lettuce) with ⅔ of the vinaigrette dressing.
5. When ready to serve, arrange leaf lettuce around the outside perimeter of the platter.
6. Rinse red pepper, cut top off to make a bowl, and remove the seeds. Very slightly, cut bottom so it will sit flat. Do not cut through bottom of pepper. Place red pepper bowl in center of platter. If you do not want to use a pepper for this, substitute a small glass bowl.
7. Around red pepper bowl, spread bibb lettuce leaves. Arrange medley of marinated vegetables on bibb lettuce.
8. Fill red pepper bowl with remaining vinaigrette dressing. Curl shrimp around top of red pepper. Serve.

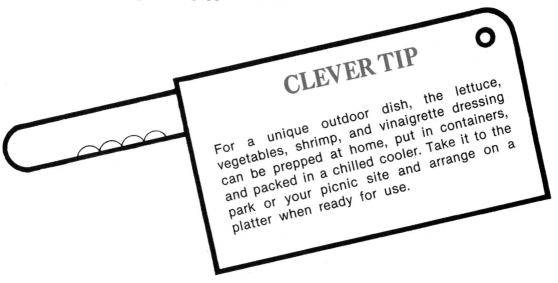

CLEVER TIP

For a unique outdoor dish, the lettuce, vegetables, shrimp, and vinaigrette dressing can be prepped at home, put in containers, and packed in a chilled cooler. Take it to the park or your picnic site and arrange on a platter when ready for use.

MARINATED HEARTS OF PALM WITH PROSCIUTTO HAM
20 hors d'oeuvres

1 can hearts of palm
1 cup Italian dressing

10 thin slices prosciutto ham,
cut in half lengthwise
20 plastic toothpicks

1. Drain the hearts of palm and discard the liquid.
2. Slice each heart of palm stalk into 4 round pieces.
3. In refrigerator, marinate the hearts of palm pieces in the Italian dressing for at least 1 hour prior to use.
4. Remove the hearts of palm from the Italian dressing.
   NOTE: You can use the drained Italian dressing for a salad or other use.
5. Place 1 piece of the marinated hearts of palm at the end of a half-slice of ham.
6. Roll so that the ham rolls around the hearts of palm piece.
7. Fasten with a plastic toothpick. Do this for all the pieces.
8. Serve on a platter with the toothpicks sticking up in the air for grabbing.

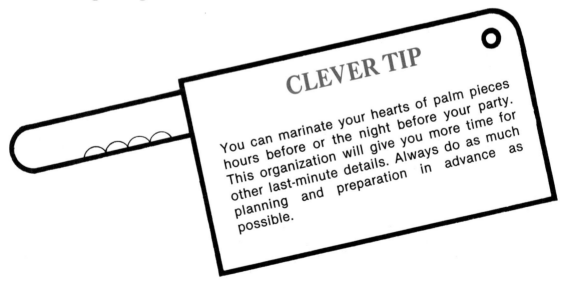

CLEVER TIP

You can marinate your hearts of palm pieces hours before or the night before your party. This organization will give you more time for other last-minute details. Always do as much planning and preparation in advance as possible.

BRIE EN CROÛTE
4–6 portions

1 small wheel of Brie
½ red Delicious apple, cored
* and sliced*
½ cup slivered almonds

1 sheet puff pastry dough
(found in the frozen food
section of your market; each
box contains 2 sheets)

1. Preheat oven to 350 degrees. Slice the wheel of Brie in half crosswise to give 2 round pieces. (Cut the Brie the same way you cut a roll for a sandwich.)
2. Layer the bottom Brie half with the apple slices and slivered almonds.
3. Cover with the top piece of Brie.
4. Spread 1 sheet of puff pastry on a cutting board.
5. Place the stuffed Brie in the center of the dough.
6. Carefully pull the dough to the center to fully encrust the Brie. Be careful not to puncture the dough.
7. Turn this encrusted Brie upside-down on a sheet pan so that the seams are on the bottom.
8. Bake on the center rack of the preheated oven for approximately 20–30 minutes, or until golden brown.
9. Remove from oven and let set 30 minutes prior to cutting. If you do not let it set, the cheese will flow out of the dough.
10. Place it on a round serving platter with a serving knife and let your guests help themselves. It cuts like a pie.

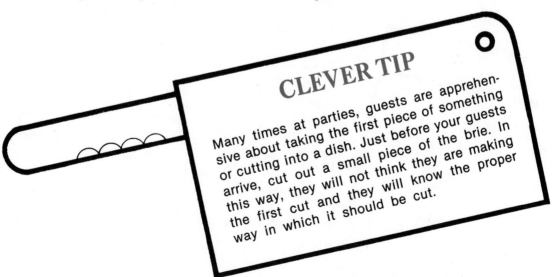

CLEVER TIP

Many times at parties, guests are apprehensive about taking the first piece of something or cutting into a dish. Just before your guests arrive, cut out a small piece of the brie. In this way, they will not think they are making the first cut and they will know the proper way in which it should be cut.

ARTICHOKE DIP
Yields 1½ cups

8½-ounce can artichoke hearts
½ cup mayonnaise

½ teaspoon garlic powder
¼ cup grated Parmesan cheese
Your favorite crackers

1. Drain and discard the juice from can of artichoke hearts.
2. Chop the artichoke hearts into pieces approximately ½ inch in size.
3. Place in a bowl and mix with the mayonnaise, garlic powder, and Parmesan cheese.
4. Mix this using the back of the spoon to break apart the artichoke pieces, still leaving them chunky.
5. Transfer dip to an ovenproof glass bowl that looks nice enough to use as a serving dish. Place this bowl in the refrigerator until you are ready to serve it.
6. For service, heat dip for approximately 10 minutes in a 325-degree oven, or just until warm. DO NOT HEAT 'TIL HOT! This will cause the mayonnaise to separate.
7. Place this warmed bowl of artichoke dip on a serving platter and surround it with your favorite crackers.

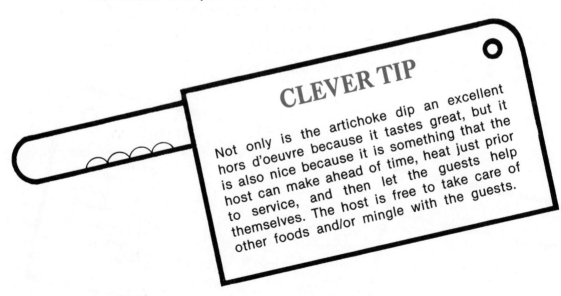

CLEVER TIP

Not only is the artichoke dip an excellent hors d'oeuvre because it tastes great, but it is also nice because it is something that the host can make ahead of time, heat just prior to service, and then let the guests help themselves. The host is free to take care of other foods and/or mingle with the guests.

LETTUCE AND CURRY SOUP
2–4 portions

½ head iceberg lettuce, cut into
 1-inch pieces
½ head romaine lettuce, cut into
 1-inch pieces
½ medium Spanish onion, cut
 into ¼-inch strips

3 cups chicken broth
Few dashes bitters
¼ teaspoon salt
½ teaspoon black pepper
1 teaspoon curry powder

1. In a large saucepan, place lettuces, onion, chicken broth, and bitters.
2. Bring to a boil, reduce to a simmer, and cook covered for 15 minutes.
3. Incorporate salt, pepper, and curry powder into soup.
4. Blend mixture in a blender or a food mill, leaving some texture to the lettuce. When doing this in a blender, be careful to do it slowly, stopping the machine occasionally and opening the top to release built-up steam. Otherwise the pressure may force hot soup out of the blender.

Our first episode on the new kitchen set.
Halfway into the show we couldn't get the
stove to light. Maybe we should have
read the instructions.

POTATO AND LEEK SOUP
2–4 portions

1 tablespoon butter
1 clove garlic, minced
1 medium Spanish onion, cut in
  ¼-inch strips
2½ cups sliced, cleaned leeks
  (white part only)

3 cups chicken broth
3 cups diced potatoes
⅛ teaspoon salt
½ teaspoon black pepper
Approximately ½ cup heavy
  cream

NOTE: Clean the leeks by cutting incisions lengthwise around the leek
       and then rinsing under cold, running water. Do this carefully, as
       leeks are a very sandy vegetable.

1. Melt the butter in a saucepan.
2. Add minced garlic, sliced onion, and sliced leeks.
3. Mix ingredients and cover pan. Let cook for approximately 1 minute.
4. Add chicken broth, diced potatoes, salt, and pepper.
5. Mix ingredients, cover pan, and bring to a boil. Reduce to a simmer
    and cook until potatoes are tender (approximately 20 minutes).
6. Blend mixture in a blender or food mill, leaving some texture to the
    vegetables. When doing this in a blender, be careful to do it slowly,
    stopping the machine occasionally and opening the top to release
    built-up steam. Otherwise, the pressure may force hot soup out of the
    blender.
7. Return blended soup back to the saucepan. Mix in heavy cream and
    adjust seasonings as necessary. Serve with a strip of the leek green for
    garnish.

CHILLED BLUEBERRY SOUP
4 portions

1¾ cups cold water
⅜ cup minute tapioca
2 cups blueberries (fresh or frozen)
1 cinnamon stick
2 tablespoons sugar

Juice of one lemon
⅛ teaspoon vanilla
1½ cups vanilla ice cream, softened
Fresh whipped cream for garnish
Fresh mint leaves

1. In a 2-quart saucepan, combine water and tapioca. Let stand for 5 minutes.
2. Add blueberries, cinnamon stick, sugar, lemon juice, and vanilla.
3. Stir and bring to a boil. Turn to simmer and cook covered, for 20 minutes.
4. Uncover and discard cinnamon stick. Let mixture cool.
5. Blend mixture in a blender until smooth. Chill in refrigerator for at least 2 hours.
6. When ready to serve, whip softened vanilla ice cream into blueberry mixture.
7. Serve in chilled soup bowls. Top with a dollop of freshly whipped cream and garnish with a sprig of fresh mint.

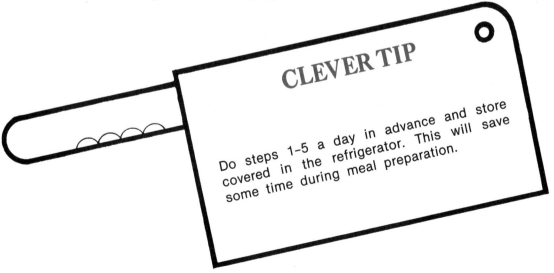

CLEVER TIP

Do steps 1–5 a day in advance and store covered in the refrigerator. This will save some time during meal preparation.

FRENCH ONION SOUP
4 portions

4 tablespoons butter
2 onions, cut in strips
2 cloves garlic, minced
1 tablespoon sugar
14½-ounce can beef broth

14½-ounce can chicken broth
½ cup sherry
1 tablespoon low-sodium
*   Worcestershire sauce*
½ teaspoon black pepper

1. In a saucepan over high heat, melt the butter.
2. Add the onions, garlic, and sugar. Mix and heat until soft and brown.
3. Add the beef broth, chicken broth, sherry, Worcestershire sauce, and black pepper.
4. Combine, bring to a boil, and reduce to a simmer.
5. Simmer for approximately 30 minutes.

Feeding "Baby Stevie."

NEW ENGLAND–STYLE CLAM CHOWDER
4 portions

3 tablespoons butter
½ onion, diced
3 stalks of celery, diced
1 clove garlic, minced
4 tablespoons flour
10-ounce can minced clams in their juice

3 cups clam juice
2 cups diced, unpeeled potatoes
1 teaspoon thyme
1 teaspoon black pepper
1 cup whipping cream

1. In a large saucepan, melt the butter.
2. Add the onion, celery, and garlic and sauté for a few minutes over medium heat. Use a wooden spoon to mix.
3. Add the flour. Mix with the wooden spoon to combine. Cook for a few minutes, stirring occasionally. DO NOT LET THE FLOUR BROWN.
4. Add the minced clams, clam juice, diced potatoes, thyme, and black pepper. Combine and bring to a boil.
5. Reduce heat and cook on a *soft* boil for approximately 15–20 minutes, or until potatoes are cooked but still firm. While chowder is cooking, stir occasionally with a wooden spoon but do not break apart potatoes.
6. Turn to simmer and mix in whipping cream. Simmer for approximately 20 minutes. ENJOY!

Our neighborhood market: plenty of credit, but tough terms.

CHILLED TORTELLINI SALAD WITH ZESTY CLEAVER DRESSING
2–4 portions

TORTELLINI

Enough tortellini for 2 people (approximately 8 ounces)

ZESTY CLEAVER DRESSING
2–4 portions

1·¾ cups salad oil
½ cup olive oil
½ cup red wine vinegar
Juice of ½ lemon
½ cup white wine
¼ teaspoon salt
1 tablespoon chopped fresh parsley
2 teaspoons chopped capers

2 teaspoons sugar
½ teaspoon minced garlic
1 tablespoon minced onion
2 teaspoons chopped fresh oregano
½ teaspoon low-sodium Worcestershire sauce
½ teaspoon Dijon mustard
¼ teaspoon white pepper
1 teaspoon chopped fresh basil

SALAD INGREDIENTS

½ red pepper, cut in julienne
½ yellow pepper, cut in julienne
20 pitted medium black olives,
  rinsed and quartered

10 Chinese pea pods, rinsed and
  cut in half
Leaf lettuce
Cherry tomatoes for garnish

STEP ONE: TORTELLINI

1. Cook tortellini until al dente (crisp to the bite). DO NOT OVER-COOK.
2. Drain and rinse thoroughly under cold water to stop cooking.
3. Hold in refrigerator for use.

STEP TWO: ZESTY CLEAVER DRESSING

1. Pour salad oil and olive oil into bowl and combine.
2. Using wire whip, slowly incorporate vinegar.
3. Add remaining ingredients and mix. Hold in refrigerator for use.

STEP THREE: SALAD

1. Gently mix approximately 1½ cups of dressing with cooked tortellini.
2. Gently mix in cut peppers, olives, and pea pods.
3. Place cleaned leaf lettuce on plates. Top with chilled tortellini salad.
4. Garnish with cut cherry tomatoes.
5. Serve immediately or hold in refrigerator for use.
6. Serve extra dressing in sauce boat.

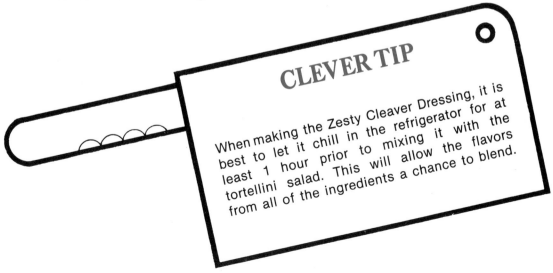

CLEVER TIP

When making the Zesty Cleaver Dressing, it is best to let it chill in the refrigerator for at least 1 hour prior to mixing it with the tortellini salad. This will allow the flavors from all of the ingredients a chance to blend.

CAESAR SALAD
4 portions

1 head romaine lettuce
2 cloves garlic, minced
6 anchovy fillets
1 large egg
2 tablespoons salad oil
2 tablespoons olive oil
Juice of ½ lemon

*⅛ teaspoon low-sodium Worcester-
   shire sauce*
2 teaspoons Dijon mustard
Pinch of salt
1 teaspoon coarse black pepper
*¼ cup freshly grated Parmesan
   cheese*

CROUTONS

3 tablespoons butter
1 tablespoon olive oil
1 clove garlic, minced

2 cups bread cubes
*2 tablespoons freshly grated
   Parmesan cheese*

STEP ONE: CROUTON PREPARATION

1. In a sauté pan, melt butter with olive oil.
2. Add minced garlic and heat just until it begins to brown.
3. Add bread cubes and toss to coat with butter. Heat until bread cubes are golden brown.
4. Place in container and mix with 2 tablespoons freshly grated Parmesan cheese. Hold for use.

STEP TWO: SALAD PREPARATION

1. Rinse romaine lettuce under cold water. Shake off excess water.
2. Cut lettuce into pieces approximately 1-inch square. Hold for use.
3. In a large salad bowl (preferably wooden), add minced garlic.
4. On a cutting board, mince anchovy fillets and, using the side of the knife, work the minced anchovies into a paste. Add to the salad bowl.
5. Add the egg to the salad bowl and, using a wire whip, mix ingredients.
6. Slowly add salad oil and olive oil. Mix.
7. Mix in lemon juice, Worcestershire sauce, Dijon mustard, salt, and pepper.
8. Add cut romaine lettuce and grated Parmesan cheese and toss to coat with dressing.
9. Add prepared croutons. Toss and serve.

It's a right hook to the jaw.

GREEK SALAD
4 portions

½ head iceberg lettuce, cut in 1-inch cubes
½ Bermuda (red) onion, cut in 1-inch strips
1 cucumber, peeled and cut in 1-inch cubes

1 medium tomato, cut in 1-inch cubes
1 cup crumbled feta cheese
6 Greek olives

1. In a large bowl, mix all of the above ingredients, except for the Greek olives.
2. Hold in the refrigerator until serving time.

GREEK SALAD DRESSING

1 cup olive oil
¼ cup red wine vinegar
1 clove garlic, minced
½ tablespoon crushed oregano

⅛ teaspoon low-sodium
  Worcestershire sauce
⅛ teaspoon black pepper

1. Mix the above ingredients to make the dressing for the salad.
2. Refrigerate for at least 1 hour prior to serving, so the flavors will have a chance to blend.
3. Just prior to service, mix the dressing with the salad.
4. Plate up the salad and garnish with the Greek olives.
5. ENJOY!

Rappin' with Regis on "Live with Regis & Kathie Lee."
WABC-TV.

BRUNCH, ANYONE?

CHEESE OMELET LOAVES
4 portions

4 small French bread loaves
1/2 pound lean ground beef
1 tablespoon chopped onion
1 clove garlic, minced
10-ounce package chopped
  spinach, moisture squeezed
  out

Salt to taste
1/4 teaspoon white pepper
8 large eggs, beaten
1 cup shredded sharp Cheddar
  cheese
1 cup shredded jack cheese

1. Cut tops from French bread loaves and scoop out some bread.
2. Sauté ground beef. When partially cooked, add chopped onion and minced garlic. Sauté until onion is translucent. Drain fat.
3. Add chopped spinach, salt, and white pepper. Combine.
4. Add the beaten eggs. Mix and cook just until the eggs are done.
5. Spoon egg mixture into hollowed bread loaves. Top with shredded cheeses.
6. Place in oven to melt cheese. Serve hot.

PUFFED APPLE JACKS
4 portions

4 large eggs
1 cup milk
1 rounded cup of flour
2 teaspoons sugar
1/2 teaspoon cinnamon

4 tablespoons melted butter
1 Delicious apple, cored, sliced
  thin, and mixed with
  2 tablespoons lemon juice and
  1/4 cup brown sugar

1. Preheat oven to 425 degrees. Beat eggs with milk in a bowl.
2. Mix in dry ingredients. Do not overmix. Leave lumpy.
3. Coat 4 casserole dishes (1 1/2-cup size) with melted butter.
4. Divide batter between 4 casserole dishes.
5. Place 3–4 slices of brown-sugared apples over top of each.
6. Place in preheated oven.
7. Bake for approximately 15–20 minutes. Serve with maple syrup.

BROILED GRAPEFRUIT
2–4 portions

2 large or 4 small grapefruit
4 tablespoons brown sugar

4 teaspoons melted butter
Few dashes bitters

1. Plane bottom of grapefruit so it sits flat.
2. Using knife, cut around grapefruit in a zigzag pattern to look like a crown.
3. Cover meat of grapefruit with brown sugar. Drizzle with melted butter and bitters.
4. Place under broiler about 6–8 inches from heat.
5. Heat until brown sugar crystallizes (approximately 3–5 minutes).

Brunch, Clever Cleaver style.

STEVE'S OMELET
1 portion

1 tablespoon butter	*1 slice of ham, diced*
¼ medium green pepper, diced	*3 eggs, beaten*
1 tablespoon diced onion	*1 tablespoon milk*

1. In omelet pan, heat ½ tablespoon of butter over medium heat.
2. Add diced green pepper and diced onion and move in pan.
3. When onion begins to become translucent, add diced ham and heat for approximately 30 seconds.
4. Add remaining ½ tablespoon of butter to pan. Move the pan so the butter will coat the bottom of the pan.
5. Add the eggs which have been beaten with the milk.
6. Using a rubber or wooden spatula, pull cooked egg to the center of the pan to allow uncooked egg to touch pan.
7. Turn omelet over in pan to cook the other side.
8. When underside is firm, fold omelet onto a warm plate.
9. Serve with your favorite breakfast items.

FRENCH TOAST
2 portions

2 eggs
2 tablespoons milk
¼ teaspoon cinnamon

¼ teaspoon nutmeg
2 tablespoons butter
4 slices bread, cut in half

1. In a small bowl, beat eggs with milk, cinnamon, and nutmeg.
2. In a sauté pan, heat butter over medium heat until hot.
3. Dip both sides of bread in egg batter. Place in hot pan.
4. Cook until golden brown. Turn and cook until golden brown on the other side.
5. Shingle half-slices of French toast on warm plates.
6. Serve with syrup and accompanying items.

Waking up with The Cleavers.

FRENCH-TOASTED SANDWICH
2 sandwiches

Whites from 2 large eggs
1 tablespoon nonfat milk
Pinch of cinnamon
Pinch of nutmeg
Couple dashes bitters

4 slices whole wheat bread
4 slices jack cheese
4 thin slices of ham
4 thin slices of turkey
2 tablespoons margarine

1. In a bowl, whip egg whites, milk, cinnamon, nutmeg, and bitters together to make a French toast batter.
2. For each sandwich to be made, take a slice of whole wheat bread and place a slice of jack cheese on it. On the jack cheese place a slice of ham, 2 slices of turkey, another slice of ham, and a second slice of jack cheese. Top with another slice of whole wheat bread.
3. Do this for each sandwich to be made. Cut the finished sandwiches in half diagonally.
4. Place the margarine in a sauté pan over medium heat. When hot, dip the sandwich half in the French toast batter and immediately put it in the hot pan.
5. Do this for as many sandwiches as you are making, or for as many as will fit comfortably in the pan at one time.
6. Cook until golden brown on both sides and the cheese is melted.
7. Cut in half again and arrange the 4 sandwich pieces on a warm plate. Enjoy with some fresh fruit slices.

CLEAVER FILE

EGGS

Eggs are graded according to quality and classified according to size:

JUMBO   30 ounces per dozen
EXTRA LARGE   27 ounces per dozen
LARGE   24 ounces per dozen
MEDIUM   21 ounces per dozen
SMALL   18 ounces per dozen
PEEWEE   15 ounces per dozen

Grading of eggs is a direct reflection of quality. Eggs are graded on flavor, thickness of the egg white, and overall appearance. The grades are U.S. Grade AA, U.S. Grade A, U.S. Grade B, and U.S. Grade C. Naturally, Grade AA is the best quality and is what we most often see in the marketplace. Grade A eggs are suitable for all uses. Grades B and C are most often used for baking.

Huey, Dewey & Louie on "The Midday Show."
KVOR TV-13 Sacramento.

MAKIN' DOUGH

CLEVERLY SIMPLE BREAD
4 loaves

2½ cups lukewarm water	*8 cups white bread flour*
1 tablespoon sugar	*2 tablespoons salt*
3 packages rapid-rise yeast	*Vegetable oil*

STEP ONE: DOUGH PREPARATION

1. Preheat oven to 400 degrees.
2. In a large stainless steel bowl, add the water. To that add the sugar and the yeast.
3. Mix with a fork, making sure all of the yeast is in the water.
4. Add the flour to the top of the yeast-water mixture.
5. Over the flour add the salt.
6. Using your hand in a circular motion, mix the ingredients. Then, use both hands to squeeze ingredients together.
7. When all the flour is incorporated, knead for 2 minutes. Shape dough into a ball.
8. Remove from the bowl and lightly oil the inside of the bowl.
9. Place dough back in bowl and press down.
10. Cover the bowl with a damp towel and place next to preheating oven. Leave it near the oven for 20–30 minutes, or until the dough doubles in size.

STEP TWO: BAKING THE DOUGH

1. Remove the dough from the bowl and place on a cutting board. Cut into 4 even pieces.
2. Lightly oil a sheet pan (approximately 11½ inches by 17½ inches).
3. Place pieces of dough, one at a time, on the cutting board. Press with the heel of your hands to flatten. Do not overwork the dough.
4. Slowly, roll the top edge of the dough towards you, pressing the edge down with each roll.
5. Continue rolling to form a French-loaf shape.
6. When rolled, pinch the bottom to seal the bread.
7. Place bread on the lightly oiled sheet pan, seam-side down.
8. Prepare the rest of the loaves in the same manner.
9. Let the bread loaves rest for 5 minutes.

10. Pat the top of the loaves *very lightly* with cold water. This will form a crust.
11. Place sheet pan on the middle shelf of the preheated oven.
12. Bake for approximately 20–25 minutes, or until golden brown.

CLEAVER FILE

When I (Steve) was a kid growing up in Connecticut, I remember my grandmother making bread and putting it under the sheets on all the beds in the house so it would rise. It was the ideal temperature. Good thing Grandma didn't work in a restaurant. I don't think they would have allowed a bed in the kitchen. But, seriously, it always amazes me when I think about some of the old methods that were used to accomplish some of the culinary tasks.

CHILI ONION BREAD
4 loaves

2½ cups lukewarm water	2 tablespoons salt
1 tablespoon sugar	Vegetable oil
3 packages rapid-rise yeast	Chili powder
8 cups white bread flour	Onion powder

STEP ONE: DOUGH PREPARATION

1. Preheat oven to 400 degrees.
2. In a large stainless steel bowl, add the water. To that add the sugar and the yeast.
3. Mix with a fork, making sure all of the yeast is in the water.
4. Add the flour to the top of the yeast-water mixture.
5. Over the flour add the salt.
6. Using your hand in a circular motion, mix the ingredients. Then, use both hands to squeeze ingredients together.
7. When all the flour is incorporated, knead for 2 minutes. Shape dough into a ball.
8. Remove from the bowl and lightly oil the inside of the bowl.
9. Place dough back in bowl and press down.
10. Cover the bowl with a damp towel and place next to preheating oven. Leave it near the oven for 20–30 minutes, or until the dough doubles in size.

STEP TWO: BAKING THE DOUGH

1. Remove the dough from the bowl and place on a cutting board. Cut into 4 even pieces.
2. Lightly oil a sheet pan (approximately 11½ inches by 17½ inches).
3. Place pieces of dough, one at a time, on the cutting board. Press with the heel of your hands to flatten. Do not overwork the dough.
4. Sprinkle the dough liberally with onion powder and chili powder.
5. Slowly, roll the top edge of the dough towards you, pressing the edge down with each roll.
6. Continue rolling to form a French-loaf shape.
7. When rolled, pinch the bottom to seal the bread.
8. Place the bread on a lightly oiled sheet pan, seam-side down.
9. Prepare the rest of the loaves in the same manner.

10. Let the bread loaves rest for 5 minutes.
11. Sprinkle the top of the loaves with chili powder and onion powder. Press it into the dough very lightly.
12. Pat the top of the loaves *very lightly* with cold water. This will form a crust.
13. Place sheet pan on the middle shelf of the preheated oven.
14. Bake for approximately 20–25 minutes, or until golden brown.

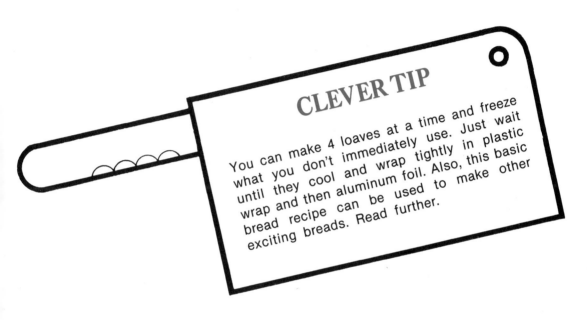

CLEVER TIP

You can make 4 loaves at a time and freeze what you don't immediately use. Just wait until they cool and wrap tightly in plastic wrap and then aluminum foil. Also, this basic bread recipe can be used to make other exciting breads. Read further.

Castaways on Cleaver Island.

MOZZARELLA AND PEPPERONI BREAD
4 loaves

2½ cups lukewarm water
1 tablespoon sugar
3 packages rapid-rise yeast
8 cups white bread flour

2 tablespoons salt
Vegetable oil
1 cup finely chopped pepperoni
1 cup shredded mozzarella cheese

STEP ONE: DOUGH PREPARATION

1. Preheat oven to 400 degrees.
2. In a large stainless steel bowl, add the water. To that add the sugar and the yeast.
3. Mix with a fork, making sure all of the yeast is in the water.
4. Add the flour to the top of the yeast-water mixture.
5. Over the flour add the salt.
6. Using your hand in a circular motion, mix the ingredients. Then, use both hands to squeeze ingredients together.
7. When all the flour is incorporated, knead for 2 minutes. Shape dough into a ball.

8. Remove from the bowl and lightly oil the inside of the bowl.
9. Place dough back in bowl and press down.
10. Cover the bowl with a damp towel and place next to preheating oven. Leave it near the oven for 20–30 minutes, or until the dough doubles in size.

STEP TWO: BAKING THE DOUGH

1. Remove the dough from the bowl and place on a cutting board. Cut into 4 even pieces.
2. Lightly oil a sheet pan (approximately 11½ inches by 17½ inches).
3. Place pieces of dough, one at a time, on the cutting board. Press with the heel of your hands to flatten. Do not overwork the dough.
4. Sprinkle ¼ cup of pepperoni evenly over each piece of flattened dough.
5. Sprinkle ¼ cup of mozzarella cheese over the pepperoni on each loaf.
6. Slowly, roll the top edge of the dough towards you, pressing the edge down with each roll.
7. Continue rolling to form a French-loaf shape.
8. When rolled, pinch the bottom to seal the bread.
9. Place bread on the lightly oiled sheet pan, seam-side down.
10. Prepare the rest of the loaves in the same manner.
11. Let the bread loaves rest for 5 minutes.
12. Pat the top of the loaves *very lightly* with cold water. This will form a crust.
13. Place sheet pan on the middle shelf of the preheated oven.
14. Bake for approximately 20–25 minutes, or until golden brown.

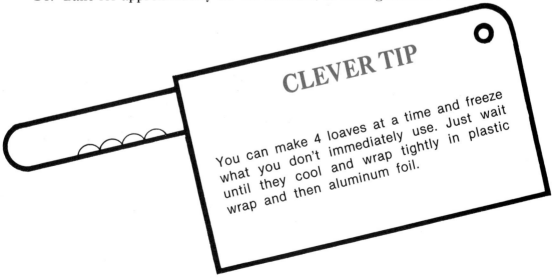

CLEVER TIP

You can make 4 loaves at a time and freeze what you don't immediately use. Just wait until they cool and wrap tightly in plastic wrap and then aluminum foil.

PARMESAN SAUSAGE BREAD
4 loaves

2½ cups lukewarm water
1 tablespoon sugar
3 packages rapid-rise yeast
8 cups white bread flour
2 tablespoons salt

Vegetable oil
1⅓ cups cooked ground Italian
  sausage
1 cup grated Parmesan cheese

STEP ONE: DOUGH PREPARATION

1. Preheat oven to 400 degrees.
2. In a large stainless steel bowl, add the water. To that add the sugar and the yeast.
3. Mix with a fork, making sure all of the yeast is in the water.
4. Add the flour to the top of the yeast-water mixture.
5. Over the flour add the salt.
6. Using your hand in a circular motion, mix the ingredients. Then, use both hands to squeeze ingredients together.
7. When all the flour is incorporated, knead for 2 minutes. Shape dough into a ball.
8. Remove from the bowl and lightly oil the inside of the bowl.
9. Place dough back in bowl and press down.
10. Cover the bowl with a damp towel and place next to preheating oven. Leave it near the oven for 20–30 minutes, or until the dough doubles in size.

STEP TWO: BAKING THE DOUGH

1. Remove the dough from the bowl and place on a cutting board. Cut into 4 even pieces.
2. Lightly oil a sheet pan (approximately 11½ inches by 17½ inches).
3. Place pieces of dough, one at a time, on the cutting board. Press with the heel of your hands to flatten. Do not overwork the dough.
4. Sprinkle ⅓ cup of ground Italian sausage over each piece of flattened dough.
5. Sprinkle ¼ cup of Parmesan cheese over the sausage on each loaf.
6. Slowly, roll the top edge of the dough towards you, pressing the edge down with each roll.
7. Continue rolling to form a French-loaf shape.
8. When rolled, pinch the bottom to seal the bread.

9. Place bread on the lightly oiled sheet pan, seam-side down.
10. Prepare the rest of the loaves in the same manner.
11. Let the bread loaves rest for 5 minutes.
12. Pat the top of the loaves *very lightly* with cold water. This will form a crust.
13. Place sheet pan on the middle shelf of the preheated oven.
14. Bake for approximately 20–25 minutes, or until golden brown.

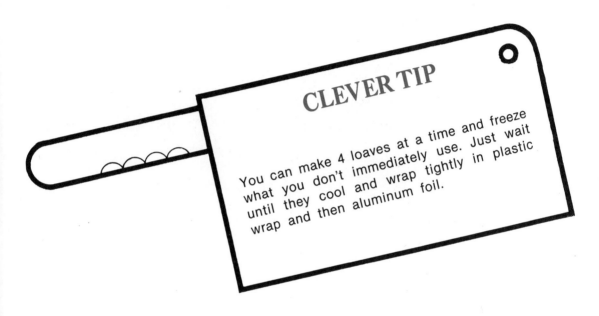

CLEVER TIP

You can make 4 loaves at a time and freeze what you don't immediately use. Just wait until they cool and wrap tightly in plastic wrap and then aluminum foil.

Don't shoot! I'm no duck.

"WHITE" PIZZA
2 pizzas (each approximately 11½ inches by 17½ inches)

2½ cups lukewarm water
1 tablespoon sugar
1 package rapid-rise yeast
8 cups white bread flour
2 tablespoons salt
Vegetable oil
½ cup olive oil

4 cloves garlic, minced
2 tablespoons crushed oregano
2 tablespoons crushed basil
1 tablespoon crushed red pepper
4 cups thinly sliced onion
2 tablespoons sugar
⅔ cup grated Parmesan cheese

STEP ONE: BASIC PIZZA DOUGH

1. Preheat oven to 400 degrees.
2. In a large stainless steel bowl, add the water. To that add the sugar and the yeast.
3. Mix with a fork, making sure all of the yeast is in the water.
4. Add the flour to the top of the yeast-water mixture.
5. Over the flour add the salt.
6. Using your hand in a circular motion, mix the ingredients. Then, use both hands to squeeze ingredients together.

7. When all the flour is incorporated, knead for 2 minutes. Shape dough into a ball.
8. Remove from the bowl and lightly oil the inside of the bowl.
9. Place dough back in bowl and press down.
10. Cover the bowl with a damp towel and place next to preheating oven. Leave it near the oven for approximately 20 minutes.

STEP TWO: MAKING THE PIZZA

1. Remove the dough from the bowl and place on a cutting board. Cut into 2 even pieces.
2. Liberally oil 2 sheet pans (each approximately 11½ inches by 17½ inches).
3. Place each piece of dough on a well-oiled sheet pan. Using the heel of your hands, press the dough out to the corners of the sheet pan and up the sides. Create an even pizza crust in each pan.
4. Rub ¼ cup of olive oil over each crust.
   NOTE: Although initially this may sound like a lot of oil, it is a necessary ingredient in the "white" pizza.
5. Sprinkle 2 minced cloves of garlic over each crust.
6. Over the garlic, sprinkle a tablespoon of oregano, a tablespoon of basil, and ½ tablespoon of crushed red pepper on each pizza.
7. Top each pizza with 2 cups of thinly sliced onion.
8. Sprinkle each pizza with 1 tablespoon of sugar.
9. Sprinkle each pizza with ⅓ cup grated Parmesan cheese.
10. Place the pizzas in the preheated oven. Bake for approximately 15 minutes, or until the crust is golden brown on the bottom. Check the bottom by lifting a corner of the crust slightly with a spatula.

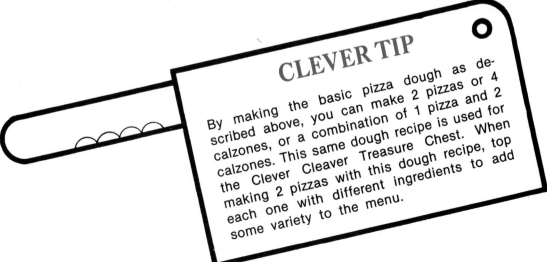

CLEVER TIP

By making the basic pizza dough as described above, you can make 2 pizzas or 4 calzones, or a combination of 1 pizza and 2 calzones. This same dough recipe is used for the Clever Cleaver Treasure Chest. When making 2 pizzas with this dough recipe, top each one with different ingredients to add some variety to the menu.

Bagging tomatoes.

VEGETARIAN PIZZA
2 pizzas (each approximately 11½ inches by 17½ inches)

2½ cups lukewarm water
1 tablespoon sugar
1 package rapid-rise yeast
8 cups white bread flour
2 tablespoons salt
Vegetable oil

2 cups tomato sauce
6 mushrooms, thinly sliced
1 green pepper, thinly sliced
1 onion, thinly sliced
7 cups shredded mozzarella cheese

STEP ONE: BASIC PIZZA DOUGH

1. Preheat oven to 400 degrees.
2. In a large stainless steel bowl, add the water. To that add the sugar and the yeast.
3. Mix with a fork, making sure all of the yeast is in the water.
4. Add the flour to the top of the yeast-water mixture.
5. Over the flour add the salt.
6. Using your hand in a circular motion, mix the ingredients. Then, use both hands to squeeze ingredients together.

7. When all the flour is incorporated, knead for 2 minutes. Shape dough into a ball.
8. Remove from the bowl and lightly oil the inside of the bowl.
9. Place dough back in bowl and press down.
10. Cover the bowl with a damp towel and place next to preheating oven. Leave it near the oven for approximately 20 minutes.

STEP TWO: MAKING THE PIZZA

1. Remove the dough from the bowl and place on a cutting board. Cut into 2 even pieces.
2. Liberally oil 2 sheet pans (each approximately 11½ inches by 17½ inches).
3. Place each piece of dough on a well-oiled sheet pan. Using the heel of your hands, press the dough out to the corners of the sheet pan and up the sides. Create an even pizza crust in each pan.
4. Spread 1 cup of tomato sauce evenly over each crust.
5. Over the tomato sauce on each pizza, spread 3 thinly sliced mushrooms.
6. Over the mushrooms on each pizza, spread the sliced green pepper and the sliced onion.
7. Top each pizza with approximately 3½ cups of shredded mozzarella cheese.
8. Place the pizzas in the preheated oven. Bake for approximately 15 minutes, or until the crust is golden brown on the bottom. Check the bottom by lifting a corner of the crust slightly with a spatula.

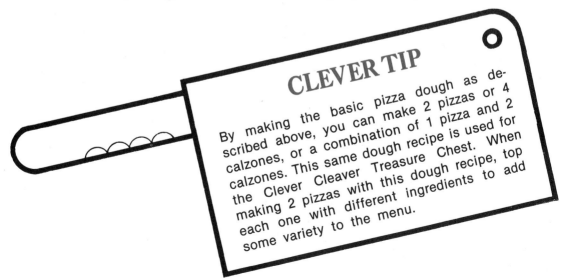

CLEVER TIP

By making the basic pizza dough as described above, you can make 2 pizzas or 4 calzones, or a combination of 1 pizza and 2 calzones. This same dough recipe is used for the Clever Cleaver Treasure Chest. When making 2 pizzas with this dough recipe, top each one with different ingredients to add some variety to the menu.

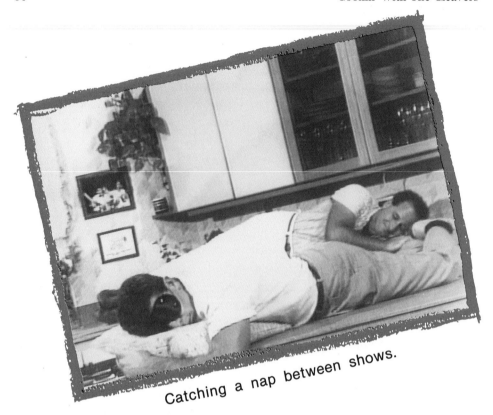

Catching a nap between shows.

ITALIAN DELIGHT PIZZA
2 pizzas (each approximately 11½ inches by 17½ inches)

2½ cups lukewarm water	*2 cups tomato sauce*
1 tablespoon sugar	*4 cups ground cooked Italian*
1 package rapid-rise yeast	* sausage*
8 cups white bread flour	*4 cups chopped pepperoni*
2 tablespoons salt	*7 cups shredded mozzarella cheese*
Vegetable oil	

STEP ONE: BASIC PIZZA DOUGH

1. Preheat oven to 400 degrees.
2. In a large stainless steel bowl, add the water. To that add the sugar and the yeast.
3. Mix with a fork, making sure all of the yeast is in the water.
4. Add the flour to the top of the yeast-water mixture.
5. Over the flour add the salt.

6. Using your hand in a circular motion, mix the ingredients. Then, use both hands to squeeze ingredients together.

7. When all the flour is incorporated, knead for 2 minutes. Shape dough into a ball.

8. Remove from the bowl and lightly oil the inside of the bowl.

9. Place dough back in bowl and press down.

10. Cover the bowl with a damp towel and place next to preheating oven. Leave it near the oven for approximately 20 minutes.

STEP TWO: MAKING THE PIZZA

1. Remove the dough from the bowl and place on a cutting board. Cut into 2 even pieces.

2. Liberally oil 2 sheet pans (each approximately 11½ inches by 17½ inches).

3. Place each piece of dough on a well-oiled sheet pan. Using the heel of your hands, press the dough out to the corners of the sheet pan and up the sides. Create an even pizza crust in each pan.

4. Spread 1 cup of tomato sauce evenly over each crust.

5. Over the tomato sauce on each pizza, spread the ground Italian sausage and the chopped pepperoni.

6. Over the meat on each pizza, spread the shredded mozzarella cheese.

7. Place the pizzas in the preheated oven. Bake for approximately 15 minutes, or until the crust is golden brown on the bottom. Check the bottom by lifting a corner of the crust slightly with a spatula.

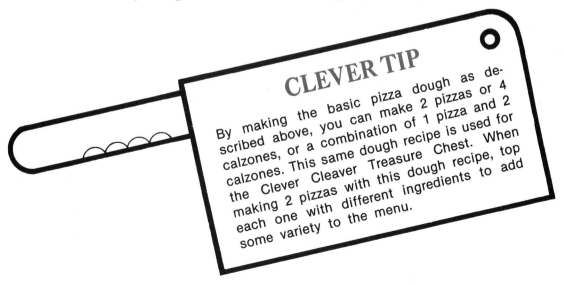

CLEVER TIP

By making the basic pizza dough as described above, you can make 2 pizzas or 4 calzones, or a combination of 1 pizza and 2 calzones. This same dough recipe is used for the Clever Cleaver Treasure Chest. When making 2 pizzas with this dough recipe, top each one with different ingredients to add some variety to the menu.

Serenading a guest.

ITALIAN MEATBALL CALZONE
4 dinner-size calzones

2½ cups lukewarm water
1 tablespoon sugar
1 package rapid-rise yeast
8 cups white bread flour
2 tablespoons salt
Vegetable oil
8 meatballs that have been browned in a sauté pan and simmered in tomato sauce

2 cups thinly sliced onion and 2 cups thinly sliced green pepper that have been sautéed in a little olive oil until the onion is lightly browned
½ cup tomato sauce
½ cup grated Parmesan cheese
1 cup shredded mozzarella cheese

STEP ONE: BASIC CALZONE DOUGH (same as pizza dough)

1. Preheat oven to 400 degrees.
2. In a large stainless steel bowl, add the water. To that add the sugar and the yeast.
3. Mix with a fork, making sure all of the yeast is in the water.
4. Add the flour to the top of the yeast-water mixture.
5. Over the flour add the salt.
6. Using your hand in a circular motion, mix the ingredients. Then, use both hands to squeeze ingredients together.

7. When all the flour is incorporated, knead for 2 minutes. Shape dough into a ball.
8. Remove from the bowl and lightly oil the inside of the bowl.
9. Place dough back in bowl and press down.
10. Cover the bowl with a damp towel and place next to preheating oven. Leave it near the oven for approximately 20 minutes.

STEP TWO: MAKING THE CALZONES

1. Remove the dough from the bowl and place on a cutting board. Cut into 4 even pieces.
2. Liberally oil 2 sheet pans (each approximately 11½ inches by 17½ inches).
3. One at a time, spread out the dough pieces into a round shape. This step can be done right on the oiled sheet pans. You can fit 2 calzones on each sheet pan. They are meal-size portions.
4. Cut the meatballs into pieces. Combine in a bowl with the sautéed onion and pepper strips, ½ cup of tomato sauce (from the pan the meatballs were cooking in), and ½ cup Parmesan cheese.
5. On each of the 4 circles of dough, cover half the circle with an equal portion of the mixture from step #4, not going all the way to the edge of the dough.
6. On top of this mixture, sprinkle each calzone with ¼ cup shredded mozzarella cheese.
7. Roll the top piece of the dough over the mixture to form a semicircular shape.
8. Turn up the edge of the dough and pinch it into the dough all the way around the semicircle. This will seal the calzone.
9. Place in the preheated oven and bake for approximately 15 minutes, or until golden brown.

CLEVER TIP

By making the basic calzone dough as described above, you can make 2 pizzas or 4 calzones, or a combination of 1 pizza and 2 calzones. This same dough recipe is used for the Clever Cleaver Treasure Chest. When making 4 calzones with this dough recipe, fill each one with different ingredients to add some variety to the menu.

PEPPERONI AND SAUSAGE CALZONE
4 dinner-size calzones

2½ cups lukewarm water
1 tablespoon sugar
1 package rapid-rise yeast
8 cups white bread flour
2 tablespoons salt
Vegetable oil

2 cups chopped cooked Italian
   sausage
1 cup chopped pepperoni
1 cup tomato sauce
1 cup shredded mozzarella cheese

STEP ONE: BASIC CALZONE DOUGH (same as pizza dough)

1. Preheat oven to 400 degrees.
2. In a large stainless steel bowl, add the water. To that add the sugar and the yeast.
3. Mix with a fork, making sure all of the yeast is in the water.
4. Add the flour to the top of the yeast-water mixture.
5. Over the flour add the salt.
6. Using your hand in a circular motion, mix the ingredients. Then, use both hands to squeeze ingredients together.
7. When all the flour is incorporated, knead for 2 minutes. Shape dough into a ball.
8. Remove from the bowl and lightly oil the inside of the bowl.
9. Place dough back in bowl and press down.
10. Cover the bowl with a damp towel and place next to preheating oven. Leave it near the oven for approximately 20 minutes.

STEP TWO: MAKING THE CALZONES

1. Remove the dough from the bowl and place on a cutting board. Cut into 4 even pieces.
2. Liberally oil 2 sheet pans (each approximately 11½ inches by 17½ inches).
3. One at a time, spread out the dough pieces into a round shape. This step can be done right on the oiled sheet pans. You can fit 2 calzones on each sheet pan. They are meal-size portions.
4. On each of the 4 circles of dough, cover half the circle with ¼ cup chopped cooked Italian sausage and ¼ cup pepperoni, not going all the way to the edge of the dough.
5. On top of the meat, dot each calzone with ¼ cup tomato sauce.
6. Spread ¼ cup of shredded mozzarella cheese over each calzone.
7. Roll the top piece of the dough over the mixture to form a semicircular shape.
8. Turn up the edge of the dough and pinch it into the dough all the way around the semicircle. This will seal the calzone.
9. Place in the preheated oven and bake for approximately 15 minutes, or until golden brown.

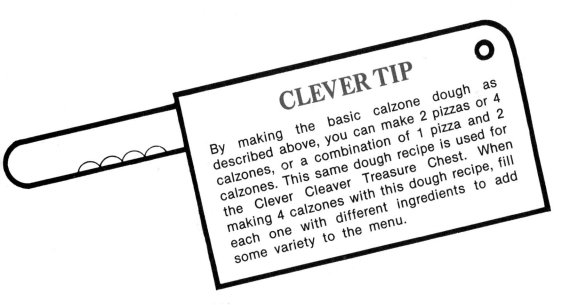

CLEVER TIP

By making the basic calzone dough as described above, you can make 2 pizzas or 4 calzones, or a combination of 1 pizza and 2 calzones. This same dough recipe is used for the Clever Cleaver Treasure Chest. When making 4 calzones with this dough recipe, fill each one with different ingredients to add some variety to the menu.

"Grey Poupon®?"

VEGETARIAN CALZONE
4 dinner-size calzones

2½ cups lukewarm water
1 tablespoon sugar
1 package rapid-rise yeast
8 cups white bread flour
2 tablespoons salt
Vegetable oil
1 cup large pitted black olives,
   quartered

2 cups thinly sliced onion and
   2 cups thinly sliced green pepper
   that have been sautéed in a little
   olive oil until the onion is
   lightly browned
½ cup tomato sauce
½ cup grated Parmesan cheese
1 cup shredded mozzarella cheese

STEP ONE: BASIC CALZONE DOUGH (same as pizza dough)

1. Preheat oven to 400 degrees.
2. In a large stainless steel bowl, add the water. To that add the sugar and the yeast.
3. Mix with a fork, making sure all of the yeast is in the water.
4. Add the flour to the top of the yeast-water mixture.
5. Over the flour add the salt.
6. Using your hand in a circular motion, mix the ingredients. Then, use both hands to squeeze ingredients together.

7. When all the flour is incorporated, knead for 2 minutes. Shape dough into a ball.
8. Remove from the bowl and lightly oil the inside of the bowl.
9. Place dough back in bowl and press down.
10. Cover the bowl with a damp towel and place next to preheating oven. Leave it near the oven for approximately 20 minutes.

STEP TWO: MAKING THE CALZONES

1. Remove the dough from the bowl and place on a cutting board. Cut into 4 even pieces.
2. Liberally oil 2 sheet pans (each approximately 11½ inches by 17½ inches).
3. One at a time, spread out the dough pieces into a round shape. This step can be done right on the oiled sheet pans. You can fit 2 calzones on each sheet pan. They are meal-size portions.
4. In a mixing bowl, combine the quartered black olives, the sautéed onion and pepper strips, the tomato sauce, and the Parmesan cheese.
5. On each of the 4 circles of dough, cover half the circle with an equal portion of the mixture from step #4, not going all the way to the edge of the dough.
6. On top of this mixture, sprinkle each calzone with ¼ cup shredded mozzarella cheese.
7. Roll the top piece of the dough over the mixture to form a semicircular shape.
8. Turn up the edge of the dough and pinch it into the dough all the way around the semicircle. This will seal the calzone.
9. Place in the preheated oven and bake for approximately 15 minutes, or until golden brown.

CLEVER TIP

By making the basic calzone dough as described above, you can make 2 pizzas or 4 calzones, or a combination of 1 pizza and 2 calzones. This same dough recipe is used for the Clever Cleaver Treasure Chest. When making 4 calzones with this dough recipe, fill each one with different ingredients to add some variety to the menu.

I think we brought the wrong bait.

CLEVER SEAFOOD CALZONE
4 dinner-size calzones

2½ cups lukewarm water
1 tablespoon sugar
1 package rapid-rise yeast
8 cups white bread flour
2 tablespons salt
Vegetable oil
½ cup grated Parmesan cheese

2 cups thinly sliced onion and
*   2 cups thinly sliced green pepper*
*   that have been sautéed in a little*
*   olive oil until the onion is*
*   lightly browned*
2 cups shredded crabmeat
1 cup shredded mozzarella cheese

STEP ONE: BASIC CALZONE DOUGH (same as pizza dough)

1. Preheat oven to 400 degrees.
2. In a large stainless steel bowl, add the water. To that add the sugar and the yeast.
3. Mix with a fork, making sure all of the yeast is in the water.
4. Add the flour to the top of the yeast-water mixture.

5. Over the flour add the salt.

6. Using your hand in a circular motion, mix the ingredients. Then, use both hands to squeeze ingredients together.

7. When all the flour is incorporated, knead for 2 minutes. Shape dough into a ball.

8. Remove from the bowl and lightly oil the inside of the bowl.

9. Place dough back in bowl and press down.

10. Cover the bowl with a damp towel and place next to preheating oven. Leave it near the oven for approximately 20 minutes.

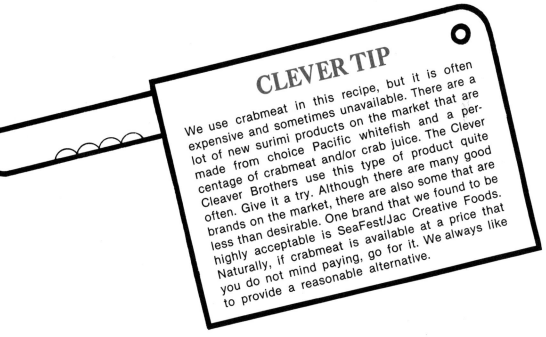

CLEVER TIP

We use crabmeat in this recipe, but it is often expensive and sometimes unavailable. There are a lot of new surimi products on the market that are made from choice Pacific whitefish and a percentage of crabmeat and/or crab juice. The Clever Brothers use this type of product quite often. Give it a try. Although there are many good brands on the market, there are also some that are less than desirable. One brand that we found to be highly acceptable is SeaFest/Jac Creative Foods. Naturally, if crabmeat is available at a price that you do not mind paying, go for it. We always like to provide a reasonable alternative.

STEP TWO: MAKING THE CALZONES

1. Remove the dough from the bowl and place on a cutting board. Cut into 4 even pieces.

2. Liberally oil 2 sheet pans (each approximately 11½ inches by 17½ inches).

3. One at a time, spread out the dough pieces into a round shape. This step can be done right on the oiled sheet pans. You can fit 2 calzones on each sheet pan. They are meal-size portions.

4. In a mixing bowl, combine the Parmesan cheese and the sautéed onion and pepper strips.

5. On each of the 4 circles of dough, cover half the circle with an equal portion of the mixture from step #4, not going all the way to the edge of the dough.

6. On top of this mixture, sprinkle each calzone with ½ cup shredded crabmeat and ¼ cup shredded mozzarella cheese.
   NOTE: We did not put tomato sauce in this version so that the delicate flavor of the crabmeat would come through a little stronger.

7. Roll the top piece of the dough over the mixture to form a semi-circular shape.

8. Turn up the edge of the dough and pinch it into the dough all the way around the semicircle. This will seal the calzone.

9. Place in the preheated oven and bake for approximately 15 minutes, or until golden brown.

CLEVER CLEAVER TREASURE CHEST
1 double-crusted meat and vegetable pie
(approximately 11½ inches by 17½ inches)

2½ cups lukewarm water
1 tablespoon sugar
1 package rapid-rise yeast
8 cups white bread flour
2 tablespoons salt
Vegetable oil
2 potatoes, quartered, sliced
  thin, and lightly sautéed in
  ¼ cup olive oil until browned

4 cups small broccoli pieces (stems
  and florets) that have been
  blanched and cooled
3 cups chopped cooked Italian
  sausage
2 cloves garlic, minced
⅓ cup grated Parmesan cheese

STEP ONE: BASIC TREASURE CHEST DOUGH
(same as pizza and calzone dough)

1. Preheat oven to 400 degrees.
2. In a large stainless steel bowl, add the water. To that add the sugar and the yeast.
3. Mix with a fork, making sure all of the yeast is in the water.
4. Add the flour to the top of the yeast-water mixture.
5. Over the flour add the salt.
6. Using your hand in a circular motion, mix the ingredients. Then, use both hands to squeeze ingredients together.
7. When all the flour is incorporated, knead for 2 minutes. Shape dough into a ball.
8. Remove from the bowl and lightly oil the inside of the bowl.
9. Place dough back in bowl and press down.
10. Cover the bowl with a damp towel and place next to preheating oven. Leave it near the oven for approximately 20 minutes.

STEP TWO: MAKING THE TREASURE CHEST

1. Remove the dough from the bowl and place on a cutting board. Cut into 2 even pieces.
2. Liberally oil 2 sheet pans (each approximately 11½ inches by 17½ inches).
3. Place each piece of dough on a well-oiled sheet pan. Using the heel of your hands, press the dough out to the corners of the sheet pans and up the sides. Create an even crust in each pan.

4. In a mixing bowl, combine the sautéed potato pieces (first drain the excess olive oil), the blanched and cooled broccoli pieces, cooked Italian sausage chunks, minced garlic, and the grated Parmesan cheese.

5. Spread the mixture from step #4 over the entire surface of *1* sheet pan of dough.

6. Invert the second sheet pan of dough over this mixture. Remove the sheet pan to leave an exposed upper crust.

7. Pinch around the 4 sides of the dough to enclose the crust.

8. Place in the preheated oven and bake for approximately 20 minutes, or until golden brown.

9. Remove from oven. Cut into square pieces and enjoy this pie.

CLEAVER FILE

We call this dish the Clever Cleaver Treasure Chest. However, its real name is pronounced *barnard.* This recipe is an old Italian favorite. We attempted to conduct some research and ascertain the correct spelling, in case it is something other than barnard, but nobody could give us anything further. They just knew that they have always called it barnard and they have been enjoying its simple and delicious appeal since who knows when. Well, if that's good enough for tradition, it's good enough for The Clever Cleaver Brothers.

Having fun with Stephanie Edwards on "L.A. in the Morning." KCAL TV-9 Los Angeles.

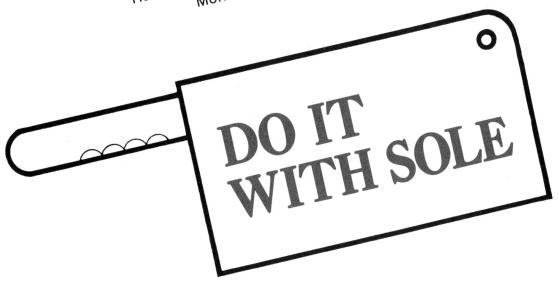

DO IT WITH SOLE

SHRIMP IN COGNAC SAUCE
2 portions

2 tablespoons butter
2 cloves garlic, minced
16 large shrimp, peeled and
  deveined
1/3 cup cognac

1/2 cup whipping cream
Few dashes bitters
2 teaspoons Dijon mustard
1 tablespoon chopped parsley
Pinch of coarse black pepper

1. In a sauté pan, heat butter over medium heat.
2. Add minced garlic and heat for approximately 30 seconds.
3. Add shrimp and cook for *approximately* 1 minute on each side.
   DO NOT OVERCOOK.
   NOTE: Shrimp will continue to cook in sauce.
4. *Pull pan away from heat* and CAREFULLY ignite with cognac.
5. When flame goes out, add whipping cream, bitters, Dijon mustard, chopped parsley, and pepper.
6. Heat until sauce is slightly thickened.
7. Serve with accompanying vegetables. ENJOY!

Quick! Where's the fire extinguisher?

CLEVER SHRIMP DIEGO
2 portions

1 tablespoon butter
1 tablespoon olive oil
2 cloves garlic, minced
16 large shrimp, peeled,
  deveined, tails removed, and
  rinsed
¼ cup cognac
Few dashes bitters

2 tablespoons chopped cilantro
½ cup green chile salsa
Salt and pepper to taste
3 cups cooked rice
Flour tortillas
Chopped tomatoes
Sour cream
Sliced pitted black olives

1. In a sauté pan, heat butter and olive oil over medium heat.
2. Add minced garlic and heat for approximately 30 seconds.
3. Add shrimp and cook for *approximately* 1 minute on each side.
   DO NOT OVERCOOK.
   NOTE: Shrimp will continue to cook in sauce.
4. *Pull pan away from heat* and CAREFULLY ignite with cognac.
5. When flame goes out, add bitters, chopped cilantro, and green chile salsa. Combine and season to taste with salt and pepper.
6. Serve over your favorite rice recipe or place in heated flour tortillas with chopped tomato, sour cream, and sliced olives.

CLEAVER FILE

When we see shrimp at the market, among other factors, the size of the shrimp dictates its price. You can tell the size by the numeral(s) associated with the shrimp. For example, U-10 means that there are under 10 shrimp to the pound. If you see 16-20, that means you will get between 16 to 20 shrimp to the pound. The numbers 21-24 means you will get between 21 to 24 shrimp to the pound. I think you get the idea. The real tiny shrimp that we usually see on a salad bar are referred to as Angel Shrimp.

SHRIMP DIJONAISE
2 portions

2 tablespoons butter
1 tablespoon minced shallots
16 large shrimp, peeled and
  deveined
½ cup flour
⅜ cup white wine

2 teaspoons Dijon mustard
Pinch of chopped parsley
Few dashes bitters
Salt and pepper to taste
1 lemon for garnish

1. In a sauté pan, heat butter over medium heat.
2. Add minced shallots and heat for approximately 30 seconds.
3. Dredge shrimp in flour and add to pan. Cook shrimp for *approximately* 1 minute on each side. DO NOT OVERCOOK.
4. Deglaze the pan with white wine. Add Dijon mustard, chopped parsley, bitters, salt, and pepper. Combine and let the wine reduce to a sauce.
5. When the sauce is slightly thickened, arrange the shrimp on the plates. Spoon sauce over shrimp and garnish the plates with a lemon crown.

AH! Shrimp Dijonaise.

GRILLED THRESHER SHARK WITH TERIYAKI SAUCE
2 portions

½ teaspoon freshly grated ginger   *½ cup grape juice*
½ cup low-sodium soy sauce   *1½ teaspoons salad oil*
1 tablespoon brown sugar   *2 pieces thresher shark*
¼ teaspoon minced garlic   *(½ pound each)*

1. Combine all sauce ingredients and hold in refrigerator for use.
2. Approximately 20 minutes prior to use, marinate pieces of shark in teriyaki sauce.
3. Place marinated pieces of shark on hot barbecue grill. Cook on both sides until shark is done (firm to the touch, with meat no longer translucent but white in color). DO NOT OVERCOOK.
4. Serve with your favorite accompanying items.

A couple of land sharks.

CLEAVER FILE

When many people see shark at the fish market or on a restaurant menu, it brings back memories of the movie *Jaws*. Although shark is still a very good value, rising prices are evidence that demand for shark is on the rise.

There are several varieties of shark available at the market. However, "The Clever Cleaver Brothers" are fond of thresher and mako shark. Thresher shark is much larger than mako and the meat is lighter in color.

Whichever type of shark you select, we urge you to try some. With the mild flavor and its good value, "The People Chefs" say, "GO FOR IT!"

BAKED COD, MACADAMIA STYLE
2 portions

2 tablespoons salad oil
2 cod fillets (4 ounces each)
½ cup flour, seasoned with salt
  and white pepper
1 egg

¼ cup crushed macadamia nuts
¼ cup white wine
Few dashes bitters
2 1-ounce butter chunks

1. Preheat oven to 350 degrees. Heat oil in sauté pan.
2. Dredge cod in seasoned flour. Dip in beaten egg.
3. Place in hot oil. Press crushed macadamia nuts on top of fish.
4. Heat on both sides until lightly browned.
5. Carefully remove fish from sauté pan and place, macadamia side up, on a sheet pan or in a pie tin.
6. Place in preheated oven for approximately 15–20 minutes. DO NOT OVERCOOK.
   NOTE: Approximately 5 minutes prior to removing fish from oven, begin sauce preparation.
7. Place white wine and bitters in small sauté or saucepan over medium heat. Bring to a boil and reduce by half.
8. Turn heat down to simmer and whip in cold butter chunks until melted.
9. Serve over fish.

Marinated scallop kebabs over seasoned noodles.

MARINATED SCALLOP KEBABS OVER SEASONED FETTUCCINE NOODLES
2 portions

MARINADE

1½ cups salad oil
Juice of 1½ lemons
1½ cloves garlic, minced

1½ teaspoons Dijon mustard
1½ teaspoons chopped fresh dill
⅛ teaspoon white pepper

1. In a mixing bowl, using a wire whip, combine salad oil and lemon juice.
2. Add remaining ingredients and mix thoroughly.
3. Cover and store refrigerated for use.
   NOTE: This step should be done at least 2 hours prior to use to give ingredients time to blend their flavors.

SCALLOP KEBABS
2 portions

1 medium red pepper	*4 medium mushrooms*
1 medium green pepper	*2 thick wooden skewers*
1 medium Spanish onion	*8 sea scallops*

1. Rinse and core red and green peppers and cut into 1-inch-square pieces.
2. Cut ends off onion and peel. Quarter onion. Pieces should be approximately 1-inch square.
3. Rinse mushrooms and cut stems flush with mushrooms.
4. In separate pans, blanch pepper pieces, onion pieces, and mushroom caps for approximately 1 minute. Cool immediately under cold, running water.
5. Holding skewer in one hand, place mushroom cap on skewer and alternate scallop, red pepper, onion, green pepper, scallop, red pepper, onion, green pepper, scallop, red pepper, onion, green pepper, scallop, and mushroom cap. Repeat with remaining skewer.
6. A couple of hours prior to use, coat kebabs with marinade and hold in refrigerator.
7. Cook kebabs over charcoal grill or under broiler until scallops are firm. DO NOT BURN OR OVERCOOK. Turn kebabs during cooking to cook evenly.
8. Serve on bed of Seasoned Fettuccine Noodles.

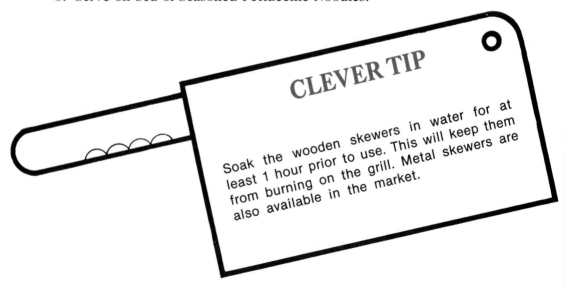

CLEVER TIP

Soak the wooden skewers in water for at least 1 hour prior to use. This will keep them from burning on the grill. Metal skewers are also available in the market.

SEASONED FETTUCCINE NOODLES
2 portions

2 tablespoons butter
1 clove garlic, minced
2 cups cooked fettuccine noodles

1 tablespoon chopped fresh basil
Pinch of salt and pepper
Grated Parmesan cheese

1. Heat butter in a sauté pan over medium heat.
2. Add minced garlic and heat for 30 seconds. DO NOT BURN.
3. Add cooked fettuccine noodles. Toss in garlic butter and heat.
4. Add basil, salt, and pepper. Combine.
5. Place on plates. Sprinkle with Parmesan cheese and place Marinated Scallop Kebabs over noodles. ENJOY.

CLEAVER FILE

Shellfish are basically members of either of two families: crustaceans or mollusks. Members of the crustacean family are lobsters, crabs, shrimp, and crayfish. The mollusk family members include scallops, oysters, and clams.

The two most common types of scallops are bay scallops and sea scallops. Bay scallops are smaller, sweeter, more tender, and more expensive than sea scallops. Bay scallops are generally used for sautéed or broiled scallop dishes. Sea scallops are larger and firmer than bay scallops.

Scallops are harvested from mid-September through the end of March. If harvesting fresh scallops, they must be mature. Two methods used to determine their maturity are: measuring the shell (it must be at least 2¼ inches in width), and looking for a dark "growth ring" that will appear along the curved portion of the shell of a mature scallop.

The scallop that we have come to love is actually the edible portion of the abductor muscle that opens and closes the shell. The important point to remember is that when harvesting fresh scallops (or any member of the mollusk family), the shell must be tightly closed. If it remains open, do not waste your time or health with that scallop. The life span of a scallop is 18 months.

When cooking scallops, regardless of the method of preparation, DO NOT OVERCOOK the scallops. They are a tender delicacy.

SOLE MEUNIÈRE
2 portions

1½ tablespoons butter
¾ pound sole (4–6 pieces)
½ cup flour, seasoned lightly
  with salt and white pepper

1 tablespoon butter
1 tablespoon chopped parsley
2 lemon slices

1. Heat 1½ tablespoons butter in a sauté pan until hot. DO NOT BURN.
2. Dredge sole pieces lightly in seasoned flour.
3. Add to pan and cook until golden brown on both sides (approximately 1 minute per side).
4. Remove fish from pan and place on plates. Put plates in warm oven.
5. Add 1 tablespoon butter to same sauté pan. Add chopped parsley and lemon slices.
6. Heat until butter just begins to brown and has a hazelnut aroma.
7. Pour over cooked sole.
8. Serve with accompanying items.

PEPPER SOLE
2 portions

1½ tablespoons butter
¾ pound sole (4–6 pieces)
½ cup flour, seasoned lightly
  with salt and white pepper
1 tablespoon butter
½ red pepper, cut julienne
½ green pepper, cut julienne

½ yellow pepper, cut julienne
1½ teaspoons green peppercorns
¼ cup champagne
⅜ cup whipping cream
½ teaspoon Dijon mustard
Few dashes bitters

1. Heat 1½ tablespoons butter in a sauté pan until hot. DO NOT BURN.
2. Dredge sole pieces lightly in seasoned flour.
3. Add to pan and cook until golden brown on both sides (approximately 1 minute per side).
4. Remove fish from pan and place on plates. Put plates in warm oven.
5. Add 1 tablespoon butter to same sauté pan.

6. When butter is hot, add julienne of red, green, and yellow peppers. Add green peppercorns and sauté for 1 minute, keeping peppers crisp.
7. Deglaze pan with champagne, and heat until most of the champagne cooks out.
8. Add whipping cream, Dijon mustard, and bitters to pan. Mix ingredients and cook until sauce thickens slightly.
9. Spoon this pepper-sauce mixture over sole. Serve with lemon crowns and accompanying items.

Sauté those pepper strips. High heat, easy on the butter.

CLEAVER FILE

Fish is classified in two categories: shellfish and finfish. Shellfish include lobsters, crabs, clams, crayfish, shrimp, scallops, oysters, and mussels. Let's talk finfish.

"The Clever Cleaver Brothers" strongly recommend including fish as a regular part of the diet. Fish is rich in protein, minerals, and vitamins. Fish is sold either fresh or frozen. If you are going to freeze fish, it should be cleaned and frozen as quickly as possible after being caught. Once frozen fish has been thawed, it should be prepared. *Never refreeze fish.* When we refer to "fresh fish," we are referring to fish that has not been frozen.

FISH

Fresh fish is sold in the following forms:

WHOLE: As it appears after removal from water
DRAWN: Entrails of the fish are removed
DRESSED: Entrails, head, tail, and fins are removed
FILLETS: The sides of the fish are cut lengthwise from the backbone
STEAKS: Cross-section slices of the dressed fish

CLEAVER FILE

Listed are some ways you can determine the quality and freshness of the fish you may want to purchase:

- Fresh fish should actually be fresh-smelling and free of fishy odors.
- The eyes should be bright, clear, and bulging. As the fish loses its freshness, the eyes will lose their clearness and will begin to sink.
- The area around the gills should be a bright, reddish-pink color.
- The scales should be bright with a sheen and should adhere tightly to the body of the fish. As the fish loses its freshness, the scales will become dull-looking and will fall off the fish easily.
- The flesh of the fish should be firm and have some elasticity. Press it with your finger; it should spring back to shape.
- Look at how the fish is being merchandised. The display should be clean and the fish should be packed in clean chipped ice.

Oh, good, one more wish. Get me out of this scene.

BEEFCAKES

STIR-FRY BEEF OVER FRIED RICE
2 portions

MARINATED BEEF

8 ounces top round
¼ cup low-sodium soy sauce
¼ cup sherry
¼ cup chicken stock

½ teaspoon freshly grated ginger
½ clove garlic, minced
1½ teaspoons brown sugar

1. Trim fat from top round and cut into ¼-inch by 1½–2-inch pieces.
2. In a bowl, combine soy sauce, sherry, chicken stock, grated ginger, minced garlic, and brown sugar.
3. Add cut meat and hold refrigerated for use.
   NOTE: This step should be done at least 1 hour prior to use to give ingredients time to blend their flavors.

STIR-FRY MIXTURE

1 medium red pepper
1 medium green pepper
1 medium Spanish onion
1 cup bean sprouts
20 small Chinese pea pods

4 green onions,
1 tablespoon salad oil
1½ tablespoons salad oil
1 cup unsalted, skinless peanuts
½ teaspoon cornstarch

STEP ONE: PRIOR TO COOKING
1. Cut red and green peppers in half. Remove stems and seeds and cut peppers into ¼-inch-wide strips. Hold for use.
2. Cut ends off Spanish onion and cut in half. Remove skin and cut with the grain in ¼-inch slices. Break pieces apart and hold for use.
3. Rinse bean sprouts in cold water and hold for use.
4. Pull stems off Chinese pea pods and rinse. Hold for use.
5. Cut the green part off green onions. Flute the white part and hold in in ice water to be used as a garnish.

STEP TWO: COOKING

1. Heat 1 tablespoon salad oil in a large sauté pan or wok.
2. Remove beef strips from marinade and add to hot pan or hot wok. Save the marinade. Cook the meat until it is brown but DO NOT OVERCOOK. Remove meat from pan or wok.
3. Add 1½ tablespoons salad oil to pan or wok. When hot, add pepper strips, onion strips, and Chinese pea pods.
4. Heat for 1 minute and add bean sprouts and peanuts.
5. Heat for 1 minute and add browned beef strips.
6. Using a wire whip, add cornstarch to marinade. Add this mixture to the sauté pan or wok.
7. Serve over Fried Rice.

Add your marinade to the stir-fry beef.

Steve and friends sing "Happy Birthday" to Lee.

FRIED RICE

1½ cups uncooked rice
2 large eggs
2 tablespoons salad oil

¼ cup low-sodium soy sauce
1 cup chopped green onion,
green part only

STEP ONE:

1. Cook rice as per instructions on package. Cool rice and hold for use.
2. Scramble eggs and cook omelet-style until firm but do not brown. Cool, cut into strips, and then cut crosswise to dice. Hold for use.

STEP TWO:

1. In a large sauté pan or in a wok, heat salad oil until hot.
2. Add cooked rice. Stir-fry for approximately 3 minutes.
3. Add soy sauce, green onion, and diced egg. Stir-fry for a couple more minutes. Turn heat to low, cover, and hold for service.

CLEAVER FILE

BEEF

Among the characteristics by which beef is graded are texture, color, amount of marbling, flavor, and overall appearance. In the retail market we most often see prime, choice, or standard, although additional grades do exist. Beef grades include:

USDA PRIME – the best grade of meat, very tender
USDA CHOICE – excellent quality
USDA GOOD – tender, but not as pleasing as choice
USDA STANDARD – generally used in institutional cooking
USDA COMMERCIAL – generally used for commercial canning
USDA CUTTER or CANNER – often used for pet food

Different cuts of beef include but are not limited to:
CHUCK – from the shoulder area and used for ground beef, pot roast, chuck roast, chuck steak, etc.
NECK – soup stock, ground beef uses, etc.
RIB – roast prime ribs, short ribs, rib steaks, boneless rib roast
SHORT LOIN – steaks, club steaks, T-Bone steaks, porterhouse steaks, tenderloin steaks, strip steaks, etc.
LOIN END – sirloin steaks, butt steaks, etc.
RUMP – rump roast, rump steaks, etc.
ROUND – top and bottom round steaks, roasts, Swiss steaks, ground beef, etc.
HIND SHANK – same as NECK
FLANK – flank steak (London broil), stews, ground beef, etc.
PLATE – braised short ribs, etc.
BRISKET – braised and boiled brisket of beef, corned beef, etc.
FORE SHANK – same as NECK

CARNE ASADA TOSTADA WITH GUACAMOLE
2 portions

MARINADE

1 cup salad oil
2 tablespoons red wine vinegar
Juice of 1½ limes
Few dashes low-sodium
  Worcestershire sauce
2 cloves garlic, minced

1 teaspoon chili powder
1 tablespoon chopped cilantro
¼ teaspoon black pepper
⅛ teaspoon salt
1 pound flank or skirt steak,
  cut in 1-inch by ½-inch strips

1. In a mixing bowl, combine marinade ingredients.
2. Add cut meat. Refrigerate until ready to use.
   NOTE: For maximum flavor, the above steps should be done at least
   1 hour prior to use.

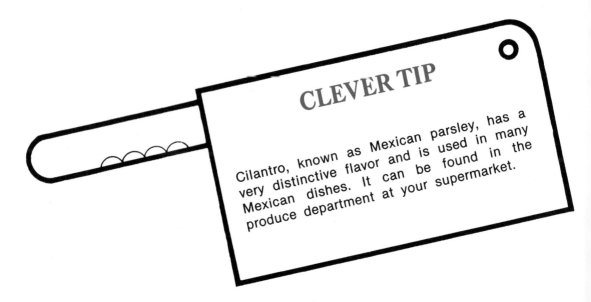

CLEVER TIP

Cilantro, known as Mexican parsley, has a very distinctive flavor and is used in many Mexican dishes. It can be found in the produce department at your supermarket.

GUACAMOLE

3 medium ripe avocados	*1 tablespoon mayonnaise*
¼ cup tomato, in ¼-inch dice	*1 clove garlic, minced*
1 teaspoon lemon juice	*⅛ teaspoon cayenne pepper*
2 teaspoons chopped cilantro	*2 tablespoons chopped onion*
Pinch of white pepper	*Pinch of salt*

1. Remove avocado meat from shell and place in a mixing bowl.
2. Using a spoon or a wire whip, work the avocado to a smooth consistency.
3. Add remaining ingredients and combine.
4. Leave avocado seed in guacamole to help keep it from turning brown. Cover and store in refrigerator for use.

TOSTADAS

Salad oil	*Shredded Cheddar cheese*
Corn tortillas	*Sour cream*
Shredded lettuce	*Guacamole*
Chopped tomatoes	*Sliced pitted black olives*

1. In a sauté pan, add 1 tablespoon salad oil and heat until hot.
2. Place a corn tortilla in pan and heat on both sides until crisp but still flexible. Do this for all tortillas to be used. Add additional salad oil to pan as necessary.
3. Hold crisped tortillas on a plate with paper towels for use.
4. When done crisping tortillas, add marinated carne asada meat to the hot sauté pan. Cook meat until done but still tender (4–6 minutes).
5. On crisped corn tortillas, place shredded lettuce, chopped tomatoes, and some cooked meat.
6. Sprinkle with shredded Cheddar cheese. Top with a dollop of sour cream and a dollop of Guacamole.
7. For garnish, place an olive slice on top of the sour cream and Guacamole. ENJOY!

CLEVER PIZZIOLA MEATBALLS
2–4 portions

1 pound ground beef
1 egg white
½ teaspoon crushed oregano
½ teaspoon crushed basil

½ teaspoon garlic powder
½ teaspoon pepper
16 slices pepperoni, chopped
Shredded mozzarella cheese

1. In a mixing bowl, combine the ground beef, egg white, herbs, and seasonings.
2. Divide the meat mixture into 8 portions.
3. In the center of each meat portion, place some chopped pepperoni and approximately 1½ teaspoons of shredded mozzarella cheese. Fold meat over the filling and shape into a meatball.
4. Place meatballs in a roasting pan and place in a preheated 350-degree oven for 20–25 minutes.
5. Place cooked meatballs in your favorite sauce and serve over pasta.

CLEVER TIP

Clever Pizziola Meatballs are an excellent dish for children. However, now that I think about it, even big kids like "The Clever Cleaver Brothers" enjoy this dish.

CLEVER KITCHEN CHILI
approximately 2 quarts

1½ pounds ground beef
1 medium onion, diced
15½-ounce can chili beans
15¼-ounce can red kidney
  beans
2 cups tomato sauce
½ cup water

1 cup red wine
2 tablespoons chili powder
1 tablespoon low-sodium
  Worcestershire sauce
1 tablespoon turmeric
1 tablespoon black pepper
2 tablespoons garlic powder

1. In a saucepan or a large skillet, heat the ground beef over medium heat.
2. When fat starts to form, mix in the diced onion.
3. When onion is translucent, drain the fat.
4. Add the chili beans, drained kidney beans, tomato sauce, water, red wine, chili powder, Worcestershire sauce, turmeric, pepper, and garlic powder. Combine.
5. Simmer for approximately 40 minutes.
6. Enjoy a bowl of chili with your favorite crackers.

Back to school with Regis on "Live with Regis & Kathie Lee." WABC-TV.

VEAL PICCATA
2 portions

1½ tablespoons butter
6 pieces boneless veal
  (8 ounces total),
  gently pounded

½ cup flour, seasoned with salt
  and white pepper
¼ cup fresh lemon juice
2 tablespoons capers

1. Heat the butter in a sauté pan over medium heat.
2. Dredge veal pieces in seasoned flour. Shake off excess flour.
3. When the butter *just begins* to turn brown, add veal pieces.
4. Cook for approximately 30 seconds on each side.
5. Add lemon juice and capers. Stir in pan to combine.
6. Place veal pieces on warm plates and top with a napé of piccata sauce from the pan.
7. Enjoy with accompanying items.

Veal Picata and Veal Marsala.

VEAL MARSALA
2 portions

1½ tablespoons butter
6 pieces boneless veal
  (8 ounces total),
  gently pounded
½ cup flour, seasoned with salt
  and white pepper

⅓ cup Marsala wine
⅓ cup whipping cream
Pinch of chopped parsley

1. Heat the butter in a sauté pan over medium heat.
2. Dredge veal pieces lightly in seasoned flour. Shake off excess flour.
3. When butter *just begins* to turn brown, add veal pieces.
4. Cook for approximately 30 seconds on each side. DO NOT OVER-COOK.
5. Remove veal pieces from the pan. Deglaze the pan with Marsala wine. (Be careful, wine may flame.) Simmer for approximately 30 seconds.
6. Add whipping cream to pan. Mix.
7. Return veal to the pan for approximately 30 seconds or until the sauce begins to thicken.
8. Place the veal on warm plates. Top with a napé of Marsala sauce and sprinkle with chopped parsley.
9. Enjoy with accompanying items.

Enhancing Medallions of Pork with a green peppercorn sauce.

IT'S SOOOW GOOD

MEDALLIONS OF PORK TENDERLOIN
2–4 portions

4 croutons
1½ teaspoons butter
1½ teaspoons salad oil
2 cloves garlic, slivered
2 sprigs fresh rosemary
6 pieces pork tenderloin, cut
  in 1-inch thickness and then
  pressed into ¼-inch-thick
  medallions

2 tablespoons Madeira wine
1 tablespoon green peppercorns
¼ cup whipping cream

1. Brush croutons on both sides with butter and toast under broiler until golden brown. This step can also be done in a sauté pan. Hold croutons for use.
   NOTE: These croutons are not salad croutons. They are cut from a piece of bread and are approximately 2½ inches in diameter.
2. Heat butter and oil in sauté pan.
3. Add garlic and rosemary. Heat for approximately 30 seconds.
4. Add medallions of pork and heat for approximately 45 seconds on each side. Remove and discard the garlic and rosemary.
5. *Pull pan away from heat* and CAREFULLY deglaze with Madeira wine. It will flame to burn off the alcohol.
6. Add green peppercorns and whipping cream. Reduce mixture until slightly thickened.
7. Place 2 croutons on each plate and top with 3 pieces of pork tenderloin. Spoon sauce over meat. Serve with vegetables of choice.

Stuffed Roast Pork Loin.

ROAST PORK LOIN
4–6 portions

½ cup diced dried apricots
½ cup diced dried figs
¼ cup diced pitted prunes
¼ cup currants
½ cup brown sugar
2 tablespoons Madeira wine

Few dashes bitters
1 boneless pork loin
 (approximately 3 pounds)
1 cup Madeira wine, divided
¼ cup whipping cream

1. Preheat oven to 350 degrees. In a mixing bowl, combine cut fruit, currants, ¼ cup brown sugar, 2 tablespoons Madeira wine, and bitters.
2. Remove pork loin from package and rinse under cold water. Pat dry.
3. Cut loin lengthwise on the side to form a pocket. Do not cut through.
4. Fill cavity with fruit mixture and tie stuffed pork loin with string every 1-inch–1½-inches.

5. Place in small roasting pan. Brush outside of loin with a mixture of ¼ cup brown sugar and ½ cup Madeira wine.

6. Place pan in the preheated oven and roast until internal temperature of meat reaches 170 degrees. This will take approximately 1½ hours. You can check for doneness with a meat thermometer or you can pierce the meat with a fork. The juice should be clear. DO NOT OVERCOOK.

7. When done, remove pan from oven. Place pork loin on a clean platter. Let set at least 20 minutes before cutting.

8. Place roasting pan over high heat and deglaze with remaining ½ cup Madeira wine. Using a wooden spatula, scrape bottom of pan to loosen browned bits.

9. When Madeira wine is reduced by half, mix in whipping cream.

10. Heat until slightly thickened. Strain and hold warm for use.

11. When ready to serve, take string off portion of pork loin to be sliced. Slice in ½-inch-thick slices.

12. Place 2 slices on each plate and lace with a napé of sauce.

13. Serve with vegetables of choice.

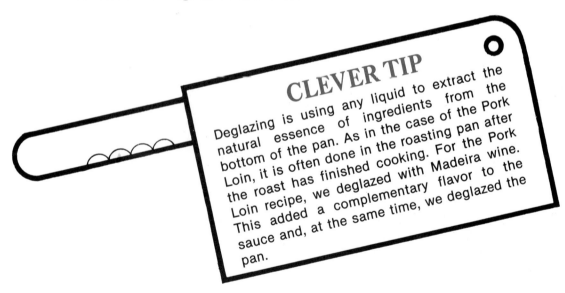

CLEVER TIP

Deglazing is using any liquid to extract the natural essence of ingredients from the bottom of the pan. As in the case of the Pork Loin, it is often done in the roasting pan after the roast has finished cooking. For the Pork Loin recipe, we deglazed with Madeira wine. This added a complementary flavor to the sauce and, at the same time, we deglazed the pan.

BAKED FRESH HAM
6–8 portions

½ cup honey
1 tablespoon Dijon mustard
¼ teaspoon grated orange zest

¼ teaspoon grated lemon zest
1 fresh ham (6–8 pounds)

1. Preheat oven to 350 degrees. In a small bowl, combine honey, Dijon mustard, orange zest, and lemon zest.
2. Leaving the netting on the ham, place ham in a roasting pan.
3. Using a pastry brush, coat ham with honey mixture.
4. Place in preheated oven. Brush with honey mixture every 45 minutes.
5. Roast until internal temperature reaches 170 degrees. If you do not have a meat thermometer, pierce ham with a fork in the center. Juice will be clear when finished. It will take approximately 2½–3 hours. DO NOT OVERCOOK.
6. Remove ham from oven and let set at least 20 minutes prior to removing the netting.
7. Slice ham for service and place on plates. Spoon a little Hot Homemade Applesauce (see p. 107) over ham slices.

Carving the ham.

STUFFED CENTER-CUT PORK CHOPS WITH APPLE BUTTER
2 portions

APPLE BUTTER
6 portions

1 large apple
Lemon juice
¼ pound (1 stick) butter,
  softened

¼ teaspoon cinnamon
1 teaspoon honey
¼ teaspoon nutmeg
¼ teaspoon lemon juice

1. Core and peel apple. Place apple in a saucepan and cover with cold water. Add a little lemon juice. Bring to a boil and reduce to simmer. Cook apple until it is soft. Remove apple and cool. Mince the apple.
2. In a bowl, combine and mix softened butter, minced cooled apple, cinnamon, honey, nutmeg, and lemon juice.
3. Spoon butter mixture down the center of a piece of plastic wrap.
4. Roll plastic wrap to form a tube shape.
5. Label and place in freezer.
6. Remove from freezer about 20 minutes prior to use so it will temper.
7. Cut in slices for use.

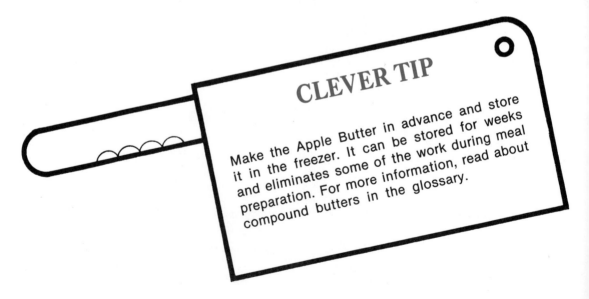

CLEVER TIP

Make the Apple Butter in advance and store it in the freezer. It can be stored for weeks and eliminates some of the work during meal preparation. For more information, read about compound butters in the glossary.

STUFFED PORK CHOPS
2 portions

2 thick boneless center-cut
  pork chops (6 ounces each)
1 tablespoon butter
1 clove garlic, minced
1 tablespoon minced onion
½ cup raisins

½ cup chopped walnuts
Few dashes bitters
¼ teaspoon allspice
1 cup bread crumbs
½ cup chicken stock
1 egg

1. Buy 2 thick center-cut pork chops or cut 2 chops from a pork loin.
2. Cut a pocket in the center of the chops. Hold for use.
3. Preheat oven to 350 degrees. In a sauté pan, heat butter. Add garlic and onion. Heat until onion is translucent.
4. Add raisins, walnuts, bitters, and allspice. Mix and transfer to a mixing bowl.
5. In the mixing bowl, add bread crumbs and chicken stock. Combine.
6. Add egg and combine.
7. Place pork chops in a roasting pan. Fill the cavity of the pork chops with the stuffing.
8. Place in the preheated oven for approximately 45–60 minutes, or until done.
9. Place cooked chops on the plates. Put a slice of apple butter on the stuffing of each chop and serve with accompanying items.

HOT HOMEMADE APPLESAUCE
2–4 portions

3 Granny Smith apples, peeled,
  cored, and diced
½ teaspoon cinnamon

3 cups water
½ teaspoon nutmeg

1. Place all ingredients in a saucepan and bring to a boil. Turn to simmer for approximately 8–10 minutes, or until apples are soft.
2. Remove from heat. Drain liquid, reserving 2 tablespoons.
3. Blend apples and 2 tablespoons liquid in blender or by hand with a whip until a little lumpy.
4. Serve warm over ham slices.

TROPICAL STIR-FRY PORK

STIR-FRY PORK
4 portions

2 fresh pineapples, yielding
  2 cups pineapple chunks
3 tablespoons peanut oil
1 pound pork tenderloin,
  cut in small pieces
1/2 cup cornstarch
1 red pepper, cut in 1/4-inch
  by 1-inch strips
20 small Chinese pea pods

8-ounce can water chestnuts,
  cut in half
8-ounce can bamboo shoots,
  drained
1/2 cup unsalted peanuts
1/2 cup shredded coconut
1/8 teaspoon white pepper
1/4 cup toasted sesame seeds

SAUCE FOR STIR-FRY

1/2 cup pineapple juice
2 tablespoons low-sodium soy
  sauce

1 tablespoon sherry
2 teaspoons freshly grated ginger
1 clove garlic, minced

STEP ONE: PINEAPPLE PREPARATION

1. Trim pineapple leaves. Cut pineapple in half lengthwise. Plane the bottom of each half so they will sit flat.
2. Cut out the hard center portion of each pineapple and discard.
3. Cut inside of pineapple halves into chunks. Remove from pineapple halves and hold for use.
4. Refrigerate pineapple boats for use.

STEP TWO: SAUCE PREPARATION

1. In a small mixing bowl, combine pineapple juice, soy sauce, sherry, grated ginger, and minced garlic. Hold for use.

STEP THREE: STIR-FRY PREPARATION

1. In a large sauté pan or wok, heat 2 tablespoons of the peanut oil.
2. Dredge pieces of pork tenderloin lightly in cornstarch. Shake off excess cornstarch.
3. When oil is very hot, add pork pieces and cook quickly on both sides.
4. Push pork to side of pan and add remaining 1 tablespoon of peanut oil.
5. Add pepper strips, pea pods, water chestnuts, bamboo shoots, and peanuts, and stir-fry for approximately 1 minute.
6. Add pineapple chunks, coconut, and white pepper. Combine.
7. Add the sauce mixture and let heat for 1 minute to thicken.
8. Place hot Curried Rice in the bottom of the pineapple boats. Spoon the Stir-Fry Pork over the rice and sprinkle with toasted sesame seeds.

Think before you wok.

CURRIED RICE
4 portions

3 strips of bacon, sliced thin   *1¼ cups uncooked rice*
¼ cup sliced green onion   *2½ cups water*
1½ teaspoons curry powder   *2 tablespoons rice vinegar*

1. In a saucepan, sauté bacon strips. When crisp, remove bacon and hold for use.
2. In hot bacon fat, add sliced green onion and curry powder. Heat for approximately 30 seconds.
3. Add rice and coat with bacon fat.
4. Add water and bring to a boil. Turn to simmer and cook for approximately 20 minutes, or until all the water is absorbed and the rice is tender.
5. Mix in crisp bacon pieces and the rice vinegar.
6. Cover pan and hold for service.

CLEAVER FILE

Although "The Clever Cleaver Brothers" did not meet until 1977, as we would later discover we had a lot in common as kids. Of course, there are a lot of people on the East Coast who could probably relate to some of our childhood experiences.

BBQs in both families were often an adventure, to put it mildly. It seems as though Mrs. Cassarino and Mrs. Gerovitz were not aware of *mise-en-place* (having everything in place prior to cooking). They would both be running to the market at the last minute for a few final ingredients. As Steve relates, the hot dogs would be coming off the grill and his family was still screaming, "Where's the mustard?" I understand that Mama Cassarino is very organized these days. I guess the Gerovitz household would be shocked if Mamma Gerovitz wasn't still running to the store just before the event.

It seems as though our dads also had a lot in common. Papa Cassarino would be doing a lot of yelling, not out of anger but, rather, in the Italian tradition. Dad Gerovitz would be yelling that he can't find any of the utensils. He'd wail, "Ever since you kids got big enough to walk, I can't lay my hands on anything."

As you can see, barbecues sure were exciting in the Cassarino and Gerovitz households.

BBQ BY THE BAY
2 portions

BBQ RIB PREPARATION
2 portions

1 slab pork ribs, cut into 2-rib
  sections
Water to cover
1/4 teaspoon salt

1/2 teaspoon celery seed
1/2 teaspoon black pepper
1/4 teaspoon liquid smoke

1. Rinse slab under cold water and cut into 2-rib pieces.
2. Place in saucepan and cover with water.
3. Add remaining ingredients and bring to a boil. Turn to simmer and cook for approximately 45 minutes.
4. Remove from pan. Let cool and coat with appropriate sauce. Hold in refrigerator until ready to use.

BBQ SAUCE
2 portions

1/2 cup chopped onion
2 cloves garlic, crushed
2 teaspoons salad oil
2 cups catsup
1 1/2 cups chopped dill pickles
Few dashes bitters

1/4 cup brown sugar
2 tablespoons dill pickle juice
1/8 teaspoon black pepper
1/4 teaspoon Tabasco sauce
1/8 teaspoon liquid smoke

1. In a saucepan, sauté onion and garlic in oil over medium heat until the onion is translucent.
2. Add remaining ingredients. Bring to boil and reduce to a simmer.
3. Simmer for approximately 45 minutes.
4. Strain sauce into container. Cool uncovered. When cool, cover and store in refrigerator for use.

HONEY MUSTARD GLAZE
2 portions

⅓ cup honey
*1½ teaspoons low-sodium soy
  sauce*

1½ tablespoons Dijon mustard
1½ teaspoons fresh lemon juice
⅛ teaspoon freshly grated ginger

1. Combine ingredients.
2. Store in refrigerator until ready to use.

IT'S BBQ TIME

1. Place ribs, coated with the appropriate sauce, on the hot BBQ grill.
2. Heat on both sides until hot and lightly glazed.
3. Whether you're having the ribs with Honey Mustard Glaze or enjoying them with BBQ Sauce, you'll be licking your fingers. Enjoy these ribs along with your favorite BBQ fare.

Beach cowboys.

CLEVER TIP

When using traditional charcoal on your BBQ grill, stack charcoal to form a pyramid. Soak with lighter fluid. When lighter fluid is absorbed in coals, carefully ignite. When coals turn gray, spread evenly. They are ready for cooking.

For some additional flavor, try using hickory and/or mesquite wood chips that have been soaked for at least 1 hour in water. Just prior to cooking, sprinkle some soaked wood chips on the gray coals. When the chips smoke, they will impart their delicious aroma on the food you are cooking. If you didn't soak the chips, they would just burn up.

CLEVEREST TIP

To try something really different and to impart a sweet aroma on your food, instead of soaking your hickory and/or mesquite chips in water, try this Clever Cleaver Find:

Fill an old, clean jar (mayonnaise type) partway with your wood chips. Pour in enough bitters to cover chips. Let soak for a couple of days. Use these soaked chips in the manner described in the above CLEVER TIP. Your food will be unique and delicious.

Two braves on the hunt.

EWE, TOO

BROILED LAMB CHOPS WITH MINT BUTTER
2 portions

MINT BUTTER
4–6 portions

*¼ pound (1 stick) softened
   butter*
*1 tablespoon chopped fresh
   mint**

1 teaspoon fresh lemon juice

1. In a small mixing bowl, mix softened butter with mint and lemon juice.
2. Spoon the mint butter down the center of a piece of plastic wrap.
3. Roll the butter in the plastic wrap to form a tube shape. Label the butter with the type and the date it was made.
4. Place butter in the freezer.
5. Remove from freezer 20 minutes prior to use so it will temper.
6. Slice the butter and place on hot lamb chops.

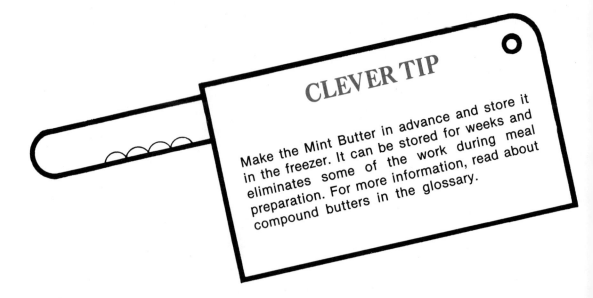

CLEVER TIP

Make the Mint Butter in advance and store it in the freezer. It can be stored for weeks and eliminates some of the work during meal preparation. For more information, read about compound butters in the glossary.

*If fresh mint is not available, use dehydrated mint. Soak it in the lemon juice so it will soften. Mix with butter.

BROILED LAMB CHOPS
2 portions

4 lamb chops   *Salt and pepper*
2 tablespoons salad oil

1. Rub lamb chops on both sides with salad oil.
2. Season lightly with salt and pepper.
3. Place in pie tin or on a small sheet pan and place under broiler approximately 8 inches from heat.
4. Cook for approximately 5 minutes per side, depending on thickness, to yield a medium to medium-well chop. Place on plate and top with slices of Mint Butter. Serve with accompanying items.

ROAST LEG OF LAMB WITH MINTBERRY SAUCE

ROAST LEG OF LAMB
2–4 portions

Boneless leg of lamb
  (approximately 1½ pounds)
1 large garlic clove, quartered

1 tablespoon olive oil
Salt and black pepper to taste
2 sprigs fresh rosemary

ROASTED TOURNÉED POTATOES
2–4 portions

3–4 large potatoes
1 tablespoon olive oil
Salt to taste

Black pepper to taste
1½ teaspoons chopped fresh
  marjoram

STEP ONE: POTATO PREPARATION

1. Cut the ends off the potatoes and quarter lengthwise.
2. Using a sharp paring knife, shape the potato quarters to form a football shape. Hold tournéed potatoes in water while doing the rest, so they won't turn brown.
3. When all the potatoes are tournéed, drain and pat dry with a paper towel.
4. Place tournéed potatoes in a bowl. Coat with olive oil and season with salt, pepper, and chopped marjoram.
5. Proceed to Roast Leg of Lamb procedure.

STEP TWO: LAMB PREPARATION

1. Preheat oven to 350 degrees.
2. Remove roast from package and rinse under cold, running water. Pat dry with a paper towel.
3. Place in a small roasting pan.
4. With a small knife, make 4 small cuts in the roast and insert the garlic pieces.

Carving the lamb roast.

5. Rub the roast with olive oil and season with salt and pepper.
6. Place two sprigs of fresh rosemary under the netting on the roast.
7. Place the seasoned tournéed potatoes in the roasting pan around the lamb roast.
8. Place the roast in the preheated oven for approximately 1 hour, or until done. Check with a meat thermometer. The roast should be 145 degrees for a medium-rare to medium roast. Adjust for your desired doneness. DO NOT OVERCOOK the roast or it will become too dry.
9. Remove the roast from the oven. Let stand for approximately 10–15 minutes before slicing.
10. Remove netting and discard rosemary sprigs.
11. Slice the roast and place on plates. Serve with Mintberry Sauce and accompanying items.

MINTBERRY SAUCE FOR ROAST LAMB
2–4 portions

1 cup whole berry cranberry
  sauce
2 teaspoons fresh lemon juice
2 teaspoons fresh orange juice

2 teaspoons chopped fresh mint
Very small pinch *of allspice*
2 whole lemons

1. Heat whole cranberry sauce in a saucepan over low heat.
2. Add lemon juice, orange juice, chopped fresh mint, and allspice. Combine ingredients and heat.
3. Make 2 lemon crowns and hollow out the inside of the lemon, leaving the bottom intact.
4. Fill the hollowed-out lemons with Mintberry Sauce. Hold in refrigerator for use.
5. When ready to serve Roast Leg of Lamb, place a lemon crown filled with Mintberry Sauce on each plate.
6. Enjoy with accompanying items.

Dining with a couple of fans.

MARINATED LAMB KEBABS
4 meal-size kebabs

MARINADE I
1½ cups

1 cup olive oil
½ cup red wine
1 tablespoon garlic powder

1 tablespoon lemon juice
1 tablespoon crushed oregano
1 teaspoon salt

MARINADE II
1½ cups

1 cup vegetable oil
½ cup red wine vinegar
¼ cup honey

1 tablespoon Dijon mustard
1 tablespoon pickling spice

1. For your lamb kebabs, make *either* marinade by mixing all of its respective ingredients in a mixing bowl.
2. Store in refrigerator for use.

CHILLED CUCUMBER SAUCE
1 cup

1 cup plain nonfat yogurt
½ cucumber, peeled, seeds removed with a spoon, and then shredded on a large cheese grater

2 teaspoons garlic powder

1. Mix the yogurt, shredded cucumber, and garlic powder in a small mixing bowl.
2. Store in refrigerator for use with the lamb kebabs.

LAMB KEBABS
4 kebabs

1 green pepper, rinsed, seeds
   removed, and cut into 1-inch
   pieces
½ medium onion, peeled and
   cut into 1-inch pieces

8 small mushrooms
4 skewers (metal or wooden)
1½ pounds boneless lamb,
   trimmed of fat and cut into
   1-inch cubes

1. Blanch the pepper pieces, onion pieces, and mushrooms for approximately 1 minute in boiling water. This is just to take the edge off the
   crispness, not to overcook the vegetables.
2. Cool immediately under cold, running water to stop the cooking.
3. On each skewer, place a piece of lamb, blanched pepper, blanched
   onion, piece of lamb, a blanched mushroom, blanched pepper,
   blanched onion, piece of lamb, a blanched mushroom, blanched
   pepper, blanched onion, piece of lamb, blanched pepper, blanched
   onion, and a final piece of lamb.
4. Do this for each of the lamb kebabs. Place in a pan and cover with the
   marinade of your choice.
5. Cover and place in the refrigerator for at least 2 hours prior to use so
   the kebabs will pick up the flavor of the marinade.
   NOTE: This can be marinated the night prior to use.
6. Place on a hot BBQ grill or under the broiler. Cook for approximately
   10 minutes or until lamb reaches your desired level of doneness.
   Baste with the marinade during cooking.
7. Remove from the grill or from the broiler and slide off the skewer onto
   plates. Serve with some Chilled Cucumber Sauce.

CLEVER TIP

If you are going to use wooden skewers, soak
them in water for at least 1 hour prior to
using, so they won't flame on the grill.

RACK OF LAMB – CLEAVER STYLE
2 portions

1 rack of lamb – 7 bones
  (approximately 1 pound)
4 tablespoons Dijon mustard

½ cup crushed macadamia nuts
  (or use crushed peanuts or any
  of your favorite nuts)

1. Preheat oven to 375 degrees. Pull the cap of fat off the rack of lamb, pulling it away from the bones.
2. Using a sharp knife, carefully remove the strip of silver skin.
3. Without cutting all the way through, make an incision along the bones. This will form a small pocket.
4. Liberally coat the inside pocket and the outside meat with Dijon mustard.
5. Put the rack of lamb in a roasting pan and coat the outside mustard area with the crushed nuts, pressing lightly.
6. Place in the preheated oven for approximately 40–45 minutes. Lamb will be cooked to the "medium" stage. Cook more or less depending on your desired doneness.
   NOTE: We recommend that you do not overcook the lamb. It is a tasty and delicate piece of meat.
7. Serve with some mint jelly or our Mintberry Sauce. Enjoy!

We will serve no wine without the mime.

MINTBERRY SAUCE
2–4 portions

1 cup whole berry cranberry sauce
2 teaspoons fresh lemon juice

2 teaspoons fresh orange juice
2 teaspoons chopped fresh mint
Very small pinch *of allspice*

1. Heat cranberry sauce in a saucepan over low heat.
2. Add lemon juice, orange juice, mint, and allspice. Combine.
3. Serve on the plate with your roast rack of lamb.

Chicky Wishbone and Mr. B. Bop Bibble.

GO FLY
THE COOP

CHICKEN WITH LYCHEE NUTS
2 portions

2 tablespoons low-sodium soy
sauce
2 teaspoons freshly grated ginger
12 lychee nuts
6–8 ounces lychee juice
(from the can)

1 tablespoon butter
1 tablespoon salad oil
2 boneless, skinless chicken
breasts, cut in strips
½ cup flour seasoned with salt and
white pepper

1. In a mixing bowl, combine soy sauce, grated ginger, lychee nuts, and lychee juice.
2. In sauté pan, heat butter and oil over medium heat.
3. Dredge chicken strips in seasoned flour and place in hot pan.
4. Sauté chicken strips on each side until done. DO NOT OVERCOOK.
5. Add sauce mixture to pan. Heat until slightly thickened.
6. Serve with your favorite vegetables. ENJOY!

"Hey, Lee, nice jacket."

CHICKEN CACCIATORE
4 portions

¼ cup olive oil
2 cloves garlic, minced
4 chicken breasts, with ribs
Salt and pepper
1 yellow pepper, cut in ¼-inch strips
1 green pepper, cut in ¼-inch strips
1 medium Spanish onion, cut in ¼-inch strips

1 clove garlic, minced
⅓ cup dry red wine
28-ounce can crushed tomatoes
¼ cup chopped fresh basil
½ teaspoon sugar
⅛ teaspoon salt
½ teaspoon black pepper
2 bay leaves

1. Heat olive oil in a sauté pan. When hot, add 2 cloves of garlic, minced.
2. Rub chicken breasts on both sides with salt and pepper. Place chicken in the sauté pan and brown on both sides. Do not try to cook all the way – just brown.
3. Remove chicken from sauté pan and place in a casserole dish.
4. To the sauté pan, add strips of yellow pepper, green pepper, and onion. Sauté for 1 minute and place on chicken in casserole.
5. Add 1 clove of garlic, minced, to the sauté pan. Heat for 30 seconds and deglaze the pan with the red wine.
6. Let the wine reduce by half and add the crushed tomatoes, chopped basil, sugar, salt, and pepper. Mix ingredients and heat for 30 seconds.
7. Place bay leaves on top of chicken. Cover with the tomato sauce.
8. Place casserole uncovered in a 375-degree oven for approximately 45 minutes or until done. Remove bay leaves and serve.

NOTE: Chicken Cacciatore can be prepared in advance. Refrigerate. Reheat slowly in a 325-degree oven.

Notice that we use a yellow pepper in this dish to give a variety of colors. If yellow peppers are not available, substitute a red pepper. If no red peppers either, use all green peppers.

CLEAVER FILE

POULTRY

All chickens are not alike. They are graded to reflect product quality and they are classified according to weight, age, and sex.

Poultry is graded to indicate the quality of its shape, flesh, and overall appearance. The grades are U.S. Grade A, U.S. Grade B, and U.S. Grade C. Most often, we see only Grade A chickens in the marketplace. Grades B and C are generally used for further processed food items such as soups, entrée dinners, etc.

Listed are the classifications most often associated with the chickens we see in the marketplace:

BROILERS OR FRYERS – average approximately 9 weeks old, weigh 1½–3½ pounds, and are tender.

ROASTERS – average approximately 12 weeks old, weight between 3½ and 5 pounds, and are tender.

CAPONS – they are castrated male chickens and generally weigh more than 4 pounds. They are tender and expensive.

FOWLS – they are mature female chickens generally weighing between 5 and 6 pounds. They are not very tender.

Stephen J. Cassarino

Stephen J. Cassarino, co-host of television's "Cookin' With The Cleavers," learned to cook both at home at his Italian grandmother's knee, and abroad under the tutelage of some of Europe's finest chefs.

"Food was always at the center of our family life," recalls Cassarino, who grew up in East Hartford, Connecticut. "Even now, I can picture all those loaves of homemade bread rising under the bed sheets and blankets on Sunday mornings ... That was Grandma's ingenious way of keeping them at the right temperature."

Cassarino, an artistic child, found cooking a natural outlet for his creativity. On the occasions when the family did eat out, he would come home and try to duplicate the dishes he enjoyed. His first such attempt, at age nine, was shrimp in lobster sauce—improvising with a can of cream of mushroom soup.

Since then, Cassarino has cooked his way around the globe, acquiring a solid classical background that is sometimes belied by his spontaneous, "down-home" attitude toward his degree from Johnson & Wales College of Culinary Arts in Providence, Rhode Island. He graduated after completing an intensive two-year program, and then worked in San Diego as a sous chef under Chef Henri Bergman at La Maison Henri.

Cassarino then studied in London under Chef Chambrette at La Petite de Cuisine in London, and in Paris under Chef Michel Pasquet at La Varenne. He managed to combine his talents with his penchant for the sea when he served as head chef for two years on a private yacht whose home port was Monte Carlo.

Before settling in San Diego, Cassarino also served as chef at the Melbourne Hotel in Brisbane, Australia, for one year.

In 1984, Cassarino teamed up with Lee Gerovitz, whom he had met at Johnson & Wales, to found Clever Cleaver Productions, a privately owned company providing products and services to the food industry. Today, the two are well known for their fun-loving approach toward television cooking as "The Clever Cleaver Brothers."

PUMPIN'
With The Clever Cleaver Brothers

Lee N. Gerovitz

It was by accident that Lee Gerovitz, co-host of TV's "Cookin' With The Cleavers," discovered his love and aptitude for cooking. During his junior year in high school, when males were finally allowed to enroll in home economics classes, he and his friends signed up on a lark for what they would call "bachelor survival class." To Gerovitz's surprise, he was hooked, and he went on to seek professional culinary training and to hold positions in restaurants both in and out of the kitchen.

Gerovitz, a native of Connecticut, graduated from Johnson & Wales College of Culinary Arts in Providence, Rhode Island in 1977. He was selected from among 600 students there to stay on for a teaching fellowship the following year. During that time, Gerovitz was chosen to assist Chef David DeWolfe with a nationwide series of National Restaurant Association seminars on soup and sauce preparation.

Gerovitz went on to become sous chef at the Opryland Hotel in Nashville, and later enrolled in Florida International University's Hotel and Restaurant Management program, receiving a Bachelor of Science degree. He moved to Thousand Oaks, California, in 1981, where he managed a Charlie Brown's restaurant for one year.

As menu development manager for the Jack-in-the-Box division of Foodmaker Inc., Gerovitz created Jack-in-the-Box's Club Pita, Pasta and Seafood Salad, and the Pizza Pocket.

Gerovitz originally met his partner, Stephen Cassarino, at Johnson & Wales, and several years later when their paths crossed unexpectedly on the beach in San Diego, they decided to go into business together. They started out with a 60-minute video cookbook geared toward beginners.

"We had no on-camera experience," recalls Gerovitz, "but we were just naive enough to forge ahead." The video was a great success and generated lots of publicity for the duo, leading to the debut of their full-fledged series.

"Cooking should be fun and spontaneous," says Gerovitz. "As a kid I watched Julia Child and was a great admirer of hers. However, I wanted our show to appeal to a different market, and to be something even beginners could enjoy."

CHICKEN BREAST OMELET-STYLE WITH CURRY BUTTER
2 portions

CHICKEN BREAST OMELET-STYLE WITH COCONUT AND ORANGE BUTTER
2 portions

CHICKEN BREAST OMELET-STYLE WITH SLIVERED ALMONDS AND RUM BUTTER
2 portions

CURRY BUTTER
4–6 portions

¼ pound (1 stick) softened butter
½ teaspoon curry powder

1 tablespoon chopped parsley

ORANGE BUTTER
4–6 portions

¼ pound (1 stick) softened butter
1 tablespoon fresh orange juice

1 teaspoon finely chopped orange zest

RUM BUTTER
4–6 portions

¼ pound (1 stick) softened butter
2 tablespoons currants soaked in 1 tablespoon of rum for 1 hour prior to use

1 teaspoon finely chopped lemon zest

1. For all butters, in a small mixing bowl, mix softened butter with its respective accompanying ingredients.
2. Spoon the mixed butter down the center of a piece of plastic wrap.
3. Roll the butter in the plastic wrap to form a tube shape. If doing more than one butter, label with type and date it was made.

4. Place butter(s) in freezer.
5. Remove butter to be used from the freezer 20 minutes prior to use so it will temper.
6. Slice the butter and place on hot chicken breast.

Compound butters enhance any dish.

CLEVER TIP

When making the Rum Butter, soak the currants in rum for an hour prior to use. The rum softens the currants and, in turn, the currants absorb some of the rum, making it easier to incorporate them into the butter.

CLEVER TIP

Make the butter(s) in advance and store in the freezer. They can be stored for weeks and this eliminates some of the work during meal preparation. For more information, read about compound butters in the Foods, Pots and Pans, and Know-How section.

CHICKEN BREAST OMELET-STYLE
2 portions

2 tablespoons salad oil
1 egg
1 tablespoon milk
2 boneless, skinless chicken
  breasts (4–6 ounces each)

¼ cup flour, seasoned with salt
  and white pepper
Shredded coconut (optional)
Slivered almonds (optional)

1. Preheat oven to 350 degrees. In a sauté pan, heat salad oil.
2. In a small bowl, beat egg with milk.
3. Trim fat off chicken breasts and dredge lightly in seasoned flour. Shake off excess flour.
4. Dip floured breasts in the egg batter and place in *hot* oil, tenderloin-side down (if it still has tenderloin attached).

OPTIONS: For coconut style, cover top side of egg-coated breast with shredded coconut, just after placing breast in hot oil. Pat coconut on breast for adhesion. For almond style, use slivered almonds and follow the procedure described above.

5. Cook for approximately 1 minute on each side, until golden brown.
6. Place on sheet pan or in a pie tin. Place in the oven for 20–25 minutes or until done, but still tender and juicy.
7. Place on warm plates. Top with 2 thin slices of your selected compound butter.
8. Serve with accompanying items.

SIMPLE STIR-FRY CHICKEN
2 portions

4 tablespoons salad oil
2 boneless, skinless chicken
  breasts, cut in finger-size
  strips
½ cup flour, seasoned
  with salt and white pepper
1 teaspoon freshly grated ginger
12 Chinese pea pods

½ red pepper, cut in strips
½ green pepper, cut in strips
⅔ cup sliced green onion
⅔ cup bean sprouts
⅔ cup unsalted peanuts
3 tablespoons low-sodium soy
  sauce

1. In a sauté pan or wok, heat 2 tablespoons salad oil.
2. Dredge chicken strips in seasoned flour and add to hot oil.
3. Cook on both sides until three-fourths cooked. Remove to a plate.
4. Add additional 2 tablespoons salad oil to sauté pan/wok. Add grated ginger, but do not burn.
5. Add Chinese pea pods and red and green pepper strips. Stir-fry in pan/wok for approximately 1 minute.
6. Add green onions, bean sprouts, peanuts, and cooked chicken strips to pan/wok and cook for approximately 1 minute.
7. Just prior to removing from heat, add soy sauce to coat ingredients.
8. Serve over Rice Pilaf.

CLEVER TIP

Notice that we use grated ginger in our recipe. Cut the bark off the fresh ginger. Grate on the small side of the vegetable grater. This will give you the ginger "pulp" for use in your recipe and leave the stringy part of the ginger behind. If you don't have fresh ginger, mix some ground ginger with the soy sauce. Taste and adjust flavor level.

CLEAVER FILE

TURKEYS

Like chickens, not all turkeys are alike. Turkeys are graded and classified.

The best quality turkey is U.S. Grade A, with the lesser quality turkeys being U.S. Grade B and U.S. Grade C. Turkeys are graded on brightness and overall quality of the skin. Skin that is torn or bruised would make it a lesser grade. Also, if the drumsticks are broken, this will make the turkey a poorer grade. Generally we see only Grade A turkeys in the marketplace, with Grade B and Grade C turkeys being used for further processed items.

Turkeys are classified as either Hen or Tom. A Hen is a female turkey and usually weighs 8–14 pounds. A Tom is a male turkey and usually weighs 16–30 pounds.

Step #1: Massage your turkey.

MAMA CASSARINO'S FAMOUS DRESSING
6–8 portions

*1 pound hot Italian sausage,
 removed from the casings
2 cups celery cut in ¼-inch
 by ½-inch dice
1½ cups onion cut in ¼-inch
 by ½-inch dice
⅜ cup (6 tablespoons) butter*

*1 bag stuffing cubes,
 approximately 14 ounces
1½ cups chicken stock
½ teaspoon sage
½ teaspoon garlic powder
2 eggs, beaten*

1. Break sausage into chunks and sauté.
2. When sausage is almost done, add diced celery and onion. Sauté until onion is translucent.
3. Add butter to the pan. When melted, add stuffing cubes. Combine.
4. Mix in chicken stock, sage, and garlic powder.
5. Cool above mixture and mix in beaten eggs to bind.
6. Dressing is now ready to stuff into turkey.

ROAST TURKEY WITH PAN GRAVY
6–8 portions

Mirepoix to cover bottom of
 roasting pan (2 chopped
 carrots, 1 onion, and 2 stalks
 celery)
1 turkey (approximately
 14 pounds)*

*Salt and pepper
1 cup chicken stock mixed with 2
 tablespoons melted butter
2 tablespoons flour*

STEP ONE: TURKEY

1. Preheat oven to 375 degrees. Cover bottom of roasting pan with mirepoix.
2. Remove giblets, neck, and liver from thawed turkey; set aside. Rinse turkey inside and out with cold water. Pat dry.
3. Rub inside cavity and outside of turkey with salt and pepper.

*See "Culinary Terms & Terminology," page 192.

4. Stuff front and rear cavity of turkey with dressing.
5. Place stuffed turkey, breast-side up, on mirepoix in pan.
6. Wrap wing tips with foil. Lightly cover turkey with foil.
7. Place in preheated oven.
8. Roast for 2 hours and remove all foil.
9. Continue to roast for approximately 1½ hours more, basting with butter and chicken stock mixture.
10. Turkey can be tested for doneness in the following ways:
    A. Drumsticks will twist freely when done.
    B. Pierce breast with a fork. Juice will be clear when done.
11. When done, remove turkey from oven. DO NOT OVERCOOK. Turkey will continue to cook for approximately 20–30 minutes after turkey is removed from oven.

STEP TWO: PAN GRAVY

1. Remove cooked turkey from roasting pan. Transfer to clean pan and cover with foil to retain heat for service.
2. Drain fat from roasting pan and place pan on heated burner.
3. With wooden spatula, scrape bottom of pan to loosen mirepoix and drippings.
4. Add 1½ cups of giblet juice mixture. (This mixture is made by placing neck, giblets, and liver in saucepan. Add 2 cups chicken stock, bring to a boil and then turn to simmer. Simmer for 20 minutes. Strain the juice for gravy and discard the parts.)
5. Bring to a boil. In a bowl, mix 2 tablespoons of flour into 1 cup of chicken stock using a wire whip.
6. Add this mixture to pan with mirepoix by pouring it through a strainer. Lower heat to simmer.
7. Adjust seasoning. Strain gravy into a sauce boat and serve with turkey.

ROAST DUCKLING
2 portions

1 Long Island duckling   *Salt and white pepper*

1. Preheat oven to 375 degrees. Rinse duck under cold water and pat dry. Cut off first and second joints of the wings.
2. Place wing tips and neck in roasting pan to act as a rack. Place duck, breast-side up, in roasting pan on wings and neck.
3. Rub duck inside and out with salt and white pepper.
4. Place in the preheated oven.
5. After approximately 1 hour, *carefully* drain grease and turn duck over. Continue to roast for an additional hour or until done.
6. Check for doneness in the following manner:
   A. When done, drumsticks should twist easily.
   B. Pierce breast with fork. Juice will be clear when done.
7. Remove from oven and let cool.
8. Split duck in half and debone each half.
9. Just prior to service, place deboned duck under broiler to reheat and crisp.
10. Place on plates and lace with a napé of Raspberry Sauce.

Flying fowl.

RASPBERRY SAUCE
2 portions

8 ounces frozen raspberries   ¼ cup whipping cream
½ cup water
Mixture of ¼ cup cold water and
   2 teaspoons cornstarch

1. Place frozen raspberries in saucepan with water.
2. Bring to boil for a few minutes.
3. Whip in cornstarch mixture. This will break apart raspberries.
4. When sauce returns to a boil, turn to simmer. Whip in whipping cream.
5. Turn off heat and cover pan. Hold warm for service.

Rowing our way into your home.

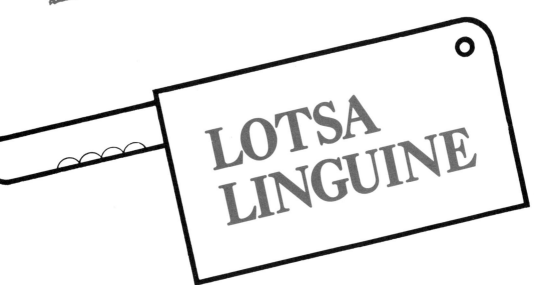

LOTSA LINGUINE

FETTUCCINE ALFREDO WITH SUN-DRIED TOMATOES AND BASIL
2 portions

*2 cups fettuccine noodles
(4–6 ounces dry)*
Salad oil
2 tablespoons butter
2 cloves garlic, minced
*½ cup chopped sun-dried
tomatoes**
*1 cup liaison (1 egg yolk lightly
beaten with 1 cup whipping
cream)*

Few dashes bitters
*½ cup freshly grated Parmesan
cheese*
2 tablespoons chopped fresh basil
Salt and pepper to taste

1. Cook fettuccine noodles until al dente. Cool completely under cold water. Oil lightly to prevent sticking and hold for use.
2. Heat butter in sauté pan over medium heat. Add minced garlic and heat for approximately 30 seconds. Don't burn.
3. Add cooked pasta and chopped sun-dried tomatoes. Combine and heat.
4. Add liaison and bitters. Mix and heat but don't allow to boil.
5. Add Parmesan cheese, chopped fresh basil, salt, and pepper. Combine and heat.
6. Enjoy with garlic bread and a green salad.

*Sun-dried tomatoes must be rehydrated prior to use. Place in a saucepan of boiling water for 1 minute. Rinse under cold water to cool and stop the cooking process. Chop for use.

FETTUCCINE ALFREDO
2 portions

2 cups fettuccine noodles
  (4–6 ounces dry)
Salad oil
2 tablespoons butter
2 cloves garlic, minced
1 cup liaison (1 egg yolk lightly
  beaten with 1 cup whipping
  cream)

½ cup freshly grated Parmesan
  cheese
2 tablespoons chopped parsley
Salt and pepper to taste

1. Cook fettuccine noodles until al dente. Cool completely under cold water. Oil lightly to prevent sticking and hold for use.
2. Heat butter in sauté pan over medium heat. Add minced garlic and heat for approximately 30 seconds. Don't burn.
3. Add cooked pasta and heat.
4. Add liaison. Mix and heat but don't allow to boil.
5. Add Parmesan cheese, chopped parsley, salt, and pepper. Combine and heat.
6. Enjoy with garlic bread and a green salad.

Clammin' with The Cleavers.

LINGUINE WITH WHITE CLAM SAUCE
2 portions

WHITE CLAM SAUCE
2 portions

1½ tablespoons butter
1½ tablespoons flour
1½ teaspoons butter
1½ teaspoons olive oil
2 cloves garlic, minced
6½-ounce can minced clams

8-ounce bottle clam juice
Few dashes bitters
1 tablespoon chopped fresh parsley
Pinch of salt
¼ teaspoon coarse black pepper

1. In a small sauté pan or a small saucepan, melt 1½ tablespoons butter.
2. Using a very small wire whip or a wooden spoon, mix in flour. This mixture is called a roux.
3. Cook on very low heat for a few minutes, stirring occasionally. *DO NOT BROWN.* Take off burner and hold for use.

4. In another sauté pan or saucepan, heat 1½ teaspoons butter, olive oil, and garlic. Heat for approximately 30 seconds.
5. Add minced clams, clam juice, bitters, and chopped parsley. Mix and heat. When it begins to boil, use a small wire whip to incorporate roux with the clams. Blend well.
6. Season with salt and pepper.
7. Serve over linguine or refrigerate for future use.

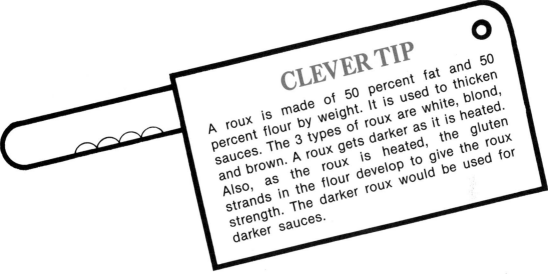

CLEVER TIP

A roux is made of 50 percent fat and 50 percent flour by weight. It is used to thicken sauces. The 3 types of roux are white, blond, and brown. A roux gets darker as it is heated. Also, as the roux is heated, the gluten strands in the flour develop to give the roux strength. The darker roux would be used for darker sauces.

LINGUINE

Enough linguine for 2 people

1. Cook linguine until it is al dente, as per the instructions on the package.
2. If ready to serve immediately, drain well and serve with white clam sauce. If linguine is for future use, cool completely under cold running water. Drain well and mix with a little salad oil to keep from sticking. Store refrigerated in a covered container for use.
3. When ready to use, place amount to be served in a colander and submerge in simmering water just long enough to heat through. Do not continue to cook.
4. Drain well and serve with White Clam Sauce.

PASTA WITH MUSSELS IN MARINARA SAUCE
2 portions

PASTA

As much pasta as needed for 2 portions

1. Cook pasta until al dente. DO NOT OVERCOOK.
2. If for immediate use, drain pasta well and serve with mussels in marinara sauce. If pasta is for future use, place in colander and cool completely under cold, running water. Drain well and mix with a little salad oil to keep from sticking.
3. Place closed container in refrigerator until ready to use.
4. When ready to use, place amount needed in simmering water just long enough to heat. DO NOT COOK.
5. Drain well and serve with Mussels and Marinara Sauce.

Place your mussels in the marinara sauce.

MUSSELS

12 mussels

1. Scrub outside shell of mussels thoroughly and pull off the beards.
2. Place mussels in a bowl, cover with cold water, and place in the refrigerator overnight or for a minimum of 3 hours. The mussels will spit out the sand.
3. Drain the water and rinse the mussels. Proceed to sauce.

CLEVER TIP

If you do not have enough time to follow the above procedure, cover the mussels with cold water and sprinkle a little cornmeal in the bowl. Let stand for 1 hour. The cornmeal agitates the mussels so they will spit out the sand. Drain, rinse, and proceed.

MARINARA SAUCE
2–3 portions

3 tablespoons olive oil

3 cloves garlic, minced

12 plum tomatoes, cored and
  cut into ¾-inch by 1-inch
  pieces

1½ teaspoons chopped fresh
  oregano

3 tablespoons chopped fresh
  basil

Salt and pepper to taste

Few dashes bitters

1 bay leaf

1 tablespoon tomato paste

½ cup water

Freshly grated Parmesan and
  Romano cheeses

1. In a saucepan, heat olive oil over medium heat.
2. Add garlic and heat just until it begins to turn brown.
3. Add chopped tomatoes, oregano, basil, salt, pepper, bitters, and bay leaf. Combine ingredients.
4. When liquid begins to form, add tomato paste and water. Combine.
5. Add cleaned mussels and cover pan. Simmer until mussels open (approximately 10 minutes).
6. If mussels open before you are ready to serve dinner, turn the burner off and keep the pan covered until ready for use.
7. Divide the cooked, drained pasta between the plates. Place the mussels over the pasta and cover with some marinara sauce.
8. Sprinkle some freshly grated Parmesan and/or Romano cheese over the pasta. Enjoy with Garlic Toast.

GARLIC TOAST
2 portions

Butter

Minced garlic

Chopped fresh basil (optional)

Chopped fresh oregano (optional)

French bread, cut in half
  lengthwise

1. In a saucepan, melt butter.
2. Add minced garlic, basil, and oregano. Heat on low heat.
3. Spoon over cut side of bread.
4. Place under broiler until golden brown.

CLEAVER FILE

Having grown up on the East Coast, we were fortunate to have experienced the fun and gratification of gathering our own mussels. Mussels use their "beard" to cling to rocks and piers and they can also be found in the mud. Be sure you can see this "beard" and make sure there is some resistance when you pull the mussel from the object to which it is clinging. This indicates that the mussel is alive. If there is no resistance, don't bother with that mussel.

Due to this nature of habitation, it is necessary to harvest mussels during low tide. Because they live in the mud and cling to objects, it is necessary to follow our recommended method of cleaning the mollusks.

We feature the mussels being served with a marinara sauce. This is delicious, but it is certainly not the only way to serve them. Sometimes, it is the simplest method that is the best. After cleaning the mussels, put them in a pot with just a little water (beer or white wine can be substituted for the water). Cover the pot and steam the mussels open. Take the mussel out of the shell and dip it into melted butter. If a mussel does not open, discard it. ENJOY!

HOT RAVIOLI WITH PESTO SAUCE

RAVIOLI

Enough ravioli for 2 people

PESTO SAUCE
2–4 portions

⅔ cup chopped fresh basil
2 cloves garlic, minced
⅔ cup olive oil
⅓ cup pine nuts (pignolis)

⅓ cup freshly grated Parmesan cheese
⅛ teaspoon salt

Lee is dangerous with an open blender.

STEP ONE: PESTO SAUCE

1. Put basil and garlic in food processor or blender. Using pulse button, slowly add olive oil and incorporate.
2. Add pine nuts and Parmesan cheese. Pulse until nuts are chopped.
3. Add salt and pulse to mix.
4. Remove from blender and hold in refrigerator for use.

STEP TWO: RAVIOLI

1. Cook ravioli until al dente. DO NOT OVERCOOK.
2. Drain and divide on plates.
3. Spoon pesto sauce over ravioli. Top with additional grated Parmesan cheese.
4. Refrigerate or freeze extra pesto for future use.

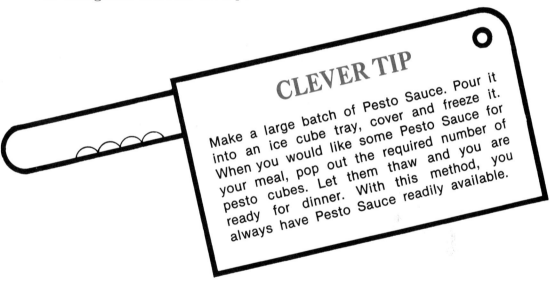

CLEVER TIP

Make a large batch of Pesto Sauce. Pour it into an ice cube tray, cover and freeze it. When you would like some Pesto Sauce for your meal, pop out the required number of pesto cubes. Let them thaw and you are ready for dinner. With this method, you always have Pesto Sauce readily available.

BAKED LASAGNA
6 portions

SAUCE

*1 pound Italian sausage
  links*
*28-ounce can whole peeled
  tomatoes*
6-ounce can tomato paste
¼ cup olive oil
2 cloves garlic, minced

*1 tablespoon chopped fresh
  oregano*
1 tablespoon chopped fresh basil
1 teaspoon sugar
⅛ teaspoon salt
1½ teaspoons coarse black pepper

1. Place Italian sausage links in a 400-degree oven for 20 minutes.
2. In a blender, place whole tomatoes and tomato paste. Cover and blend *just until tomatoes are broken*. If you do not have a blender, break tomatoes by hand and mix with tomato paste.
3. In a saucepan, heat olive oil. When hot, add minced garlic, chopped oregano, and chopped basil. Heat, but do not brown garlic.
4. Add blended tomato mixture, sugar, salt, and pepper. Mix well.
5. Add roasted sausage links. Cover pan loosely and simmer for 1 hour.
6. When sauce is done, remove sausage links to cool. Place sauce in a container and place uncovered in the refrigerator to cool completely. Cover when cooled and hold for lasagna assembly.
7. Chop cooled Italian sausage into ¼-inch dice and hold in refrigerator for lasagna assembly.

RICOTTA CHEESE MIXTURE

1 pound ricotta cheese
1 large egg
1 tablespoon chopped parsley
½ teaspoon coarse black pepper

¼ cup grated Parmesan cheese
1 clove garlic, minced
⅛ teaspoon salt

1. In a bowl, mix ricotta cheese and egg.
2. Add remaining ingredients. Hold refrigerated for lasagna assembly.

LASAGNA

1 package lasagna noodles	*Italian sausage, roasted and*
Salad oil	*chopped (see p. 150)*
Prepared sauce (see p. 150)	*4 cups shredded mozzarella cheese*
Prepared ricotta cheese mixture	
(see p. 150)	

STEP ONE: NOODLE PREPARATION

1. Cook package of lasagna noodles until al dente, as per the instructions on the package. DO NOT OVERCOOK.
2. Cool noodles completely under cold water. Pat dry with paper towels.
3. Rub noodles very lightly with salad oil and store flat in refrigerator for lasagna assembly.

STEP TWO: LASAGNA ASSEMBLY

1. Preheat oven to 350 degrees. Cover bottom of 8-inch by 8-inch baking pan with a light layer of sauce.
2. Over the sauce, place a layer of lasagna noodles. All the noodles should go in the same direction.
3. On noodles, place a thin layer of ricotta cheese mixture.
4. Next, sprinkle a layer of chopped Italian sausage and shredded mozzarella cheese. Place some sauce on various spots on the sausage and mozzarella cheese.
5. Place another layer of lasagna noodles in pan. These noodles should go in the opposite direction of the first layer of noodles.
6. On noodles, place ricotta cheese mixture, chopped sausage, shredded mozzarella cheese, and sauce, in the manner previously described.
7. Place another layer of cooked lasagna noodles in pan, going in the opposite direction of the previous layer.
8. Press noodles down with hands to pack firmly and distribute ingredients.
9. Spread a layer of ricotta cheese mixture over noodles and sprinkle with mozzarella cheese.

10. Place another layer of cooked lasagna noodles over mozzarella cheese, going in the opposite direction of the previous layer. Press down with hands to pack firmly.
11. Cover noodles with a layer of sauce and sprinkle with a layer of shredded mozzarella cheese.
12. Place in preheated oven for 1 hour.
13. Remove from oven. If for immediate use, let set for 20 minutes prior to cutting so lasagna will firm.
14. Place a little hot sauce on each plate. On sauce, place a portion of lasagna. Serve with accompanying items.

Lasagna at its best.

CLEVER TIP

Lasagna tastes great when you make it a day or two prior to its intended use. Let it cool after removing from oven. When completely cool, cover with plastic wrap and store in the refrigerator. Reheat in a 300-degree oven until hot. Let set for 10 minutes and cut for service.

CLEVEREST TIP

Regardless of how far in advance you prepare your lasagna, the procedure we describe for lasagna assembly works best when all of the ingredients are cold.

All right! Free shrimp. I'm glad I brought my teeth.

EVERYONE'S GRAZING

ROASTED QUARTERED POTATOES
2 portions

2 russet potatoes   *Salt, pepper, paprika*
Salad oil

1. Quarter russet potatoes lengthwise.
2. Rub liberally with salad oil and place in pie tin.
3. Season lightly with salt, pepper, and paprika.
4. Place in 350-degree oven for approximately 45 minutes, or until tender.
5. Potatoes should be turned once during cooking to brown evenly.

FRESH CRANBERRY SAUCE
2 portions

Water, as per instructions on   *1 tablespoon grated orange zest*
* package of cranberries*   *1 bag fresh cranberries*
Sugar, as per instructions on
* package of cranberries*

1. Place water, sugar, orange zest, and cranberries in saucepan.
2. Cook as per instructions on package.
3. Cool and hold for service.

PARSLEY RAP POTATOES
2 portions

2 large potatoes
1 tablespoon butter

Salt and white pepper
1 tablespoon chopped fresh parsley

1. Peel potatoes and rinse under cold water. Keep in cold water so they will not turn brown.
2. Using parisienne scoop, scoop out potato balls as needed. Keep potato balls in water.
3. Place potato balls in a saucepan. Cover with cold water. Bring water to a boil and turn to simmer. Cook just until potatoes are al dente. DO NOT OVERCOOK.
4. Drain and cool completely under cold, running water. Be careful not to let running water break apart potato balls. Pat potatoes dry with a paper towel. Place in refrigerator for future use or proceed to final steps.
5. Heat the butter in a sauté pan. Add potato balls, salt, white pepper, and chopped parsley. Sauté until hot. Serve.

Rock around the pot.

TOURNÉED CARROTS
2 portions

2 large carrots   *Salt and white pepper to taste*
1 tablespoon butter

1. Cut carrots into pieces approximately 1½ inches long.
2. Using a paring knife, shape pieces of carrot into tournée* shape.
3. Place rinsed tournéed carrot pieces in a pan of boiling salted water. Turn to simmer and cook until al dente. DO NOT OVERCOOK.
4. Cool immediately under cold, running water. Hold for use.
5. When ready to use, heat butter in a sauté pan over medium heat. Add cooked carrots, salt, and white pepper.
6. Heat until hot. Serve.

TOURNÉED POTATOES
2 portions

2 large potatoes   *Salt and white pepper to taste*
1 tablespoon butter

1. Cut potatoes into tournée shape.
2. Rinse cut potatoes and place in a saucepan. Cover with cold water.
3. Bring water to a boil and turn to simmer. Cook until potatoes are al dente. DO NOT OVERCOOK.
4. Drain and immediately cool under cold, running water. Hold for use.
5. When ready to use, heat butter in a sauté pan over medium heat. Add cooked potatoes, salt, and white pepper.
6. Heat until hot. Serve.

*See "Cuts and Sizes," p. 208.

BAKED YAMS
2 portions

2 yams   *Butter*

1. Rinse yams.
2. Place on sheet pan or in a pie tin and place in a 350-degree preheated oven.
3. Bake for approximately 1 hour, or until soft. Serve with butter.

SAUTÉED BRUSSELS SPROUTS
2 portions

10 Brussels sprouts   *Salt to taste*
1 tablespoon butter   *White pepper to taste*

1. Remove outer leaves from Brussels sprouts and rinse under cold water.
2. Place in boiling salted water and cook until al dente. DO NOT OVERCOOK.
3. Place under cold, running water to stop the cooking. Drain well.
4. When ready to serve, heat butter in a sauté pan.
5. Add Brussels sprouts and sauté until hot.
6. Season with salt and white pepper to taste.

RICE PILAF
2–4 portions

1 tablespoon butter	*½ teaspoon crushed thyme*
1 celery stalk, diced	*¼ teaspoon black pepper*
2 tablespoons diced onion	*1 cup uncooked rice*
½ cup sliced mushrooms	*2 cups chicken broth*
1 teaspoon crushed oregano	*2 bay leaves*

1. Heat butter in a medium saucepan.
2. When hot, add diced celery and onion and cook for approximately 1 minute.
3. Add sliced mushrooms, oregano, thyme, and black pepper. Combine.
4. Add rice and mix to coat with butter. Heat for 1 minute, stirring so rice will not brown.
5. Add chicken broth and bay leaves. Combine.
6. Bring to a boil and immediately reduce to a simmer. Cover pan.
7. Cook until liquid is absorbed and rice is tender, approximately 20 minutes.
8. Remove bay leaves, fluff rice, and cover pan. Hold rice for service.

Umm, Umm Good!

SPICED FRUIT RICE
4–6 portions

2 cups water
1 cup rice
1½ teaspoons lemon juice
2 tablespoons currants

⅔ cup diced apple
⅓ cup diced dried apricots
⅛ teaspoon cinnamon
⅛ teaspoon nutmeg

1. Place water in a saucepan and bring to a boil.
2. When boiling, mix in rice. Turn to simmer.
3. Cook for 15–20 minutes, or just until liquid is absorbed.
4. Turn off heat and fluff rice with a fork.
5. Combine remaining ingredients with rice. Cover and hold for service.
   NOTE: After doing Step #2, cut the fruit and mix with spices and lemon juice.

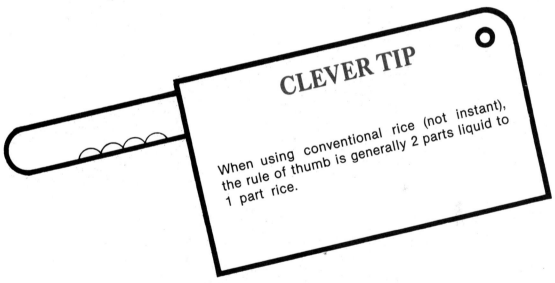

CLEVER TIP

When using conventional rice (not instant), the rule of thumb is generally 2 parts liquid to 1 part rice.

CURRIED RICE
4 portions

3 thin strips bacon	*1¼ cups uncooked rice*
¼ cup sliced green onion	*2½ cups water*
1½ teaspoons curry powder	*2 tablespoons rice wine vinegar*

1. In a saucepan, sauté bacon strips. When crisp, remove bacon and hold for use.
2. In hot bacon fat, add sliced green onion and curry powder. Heat for approximately 30 seconds.
3. Add rice and coat with bacon fat.
4. Add water and bring to a boil. Turn to simmer and cook for approximately 20 minutes, or until all the water is absorbed and the rice is tender.
5. Mix in crisp bacon pieces and the rice wine vinegar.
6. Cover pan and hold for service.

Cryovac® the Magnificent and Ed McPan.

BAKED POTATO
2 portions

2 baking potatoes   *Butter, sour cream, chives*
1 tablespoon salad oil   *(optional)*

1. Preheat oven to 350 degrees. Wash potatoes and rub with salad oil.
2. Pierce both ends of the potato with a fork to allow steam to escape.
3. Place in the preheated oven for approximately 45–60 minutes, depending on the size of the potato.
4. Test by inserting fork. If it goes in easily, potato is done. DO NOT OVERCOOK.
5. To serve, cut a cross in the top of the potato. Squeeze from the bottom to open potato.
6. Top with your favorite condiments.

GREEN BEANS ALMONDINE
2 portions

16 green beans, washed,   *1 tablespoon butter*
  trimmed, cut in half, and   *¼ cup slivered almonds*
  blanched   *Salt and white pepper to taste*

1. Cool blanched string beans completely under cold water. Do this step ahead of time and hold in refrigerator for use.
2. Heat butter in sauté pan over medium heat.
3. Add slivered almonds. Cook until they are lightly roasted. (You will smell the delicious aroma.) DO NOT BURN.
4. Add blanched green beans and season with salt and pepper to taste.
5. Heat thoroughly.

CARROTS WITH HONEY & DILL
2 portions

1½ cups sliced carrots   *1 tablespoon chopped fresh dill*
1 tablespoon butter   *Salt and white pepper to taste*
1½ tablespoons honey

1. Place carrots in boiling salted water and cook until they are al dente. DO NOT OVERCOOK.
2. Cool completely under cold water.
3. Heat butter in sauté pan over medium heat.
4. When butter is hot, add blanched carrots. Cook, stirring, until carrots are heated through.
5. Add honey and dill. Coat evenly.
6. Season with salt and white pepper to taste.

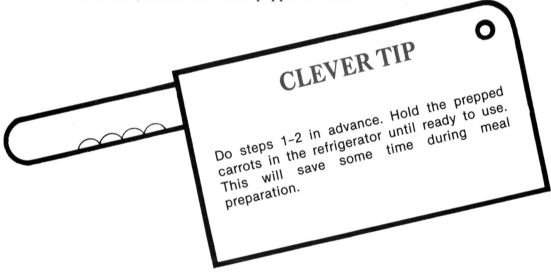

CLEVER TIP

Do steps 1–2 in advance. Hold the prepped carrots in the refrigerator until ready to use. This will save some time during meal preparation.

CARROTS WITH PERNOD
2 portions

1 tablespoon butter
1½ cups sliced blanched carrots

Salt and white pepper to taste
3 tablespoons Pernod

1. Heat butter in sauté pan.
2. Add the blanched carrots and season with salt and white pepper.
3. Heat for approximately 1 minute.
4. *Pull pan away from heat* and CAREFULLY ignite with Pernod.
5. Serve.

FRESH PEAS WITH BACON
2 portions

½ pound shelled fresh peas
1 tablespoon butter, melted

3 strips bacon, cooked and
chopped

1. Hull peas and rinse under cold water.
2. Add peas to boiling, salted water.
3. Remove when al dente. Drain and add to sauté pan with melted butter.
4. Add chopped, cooked bacon and serve.

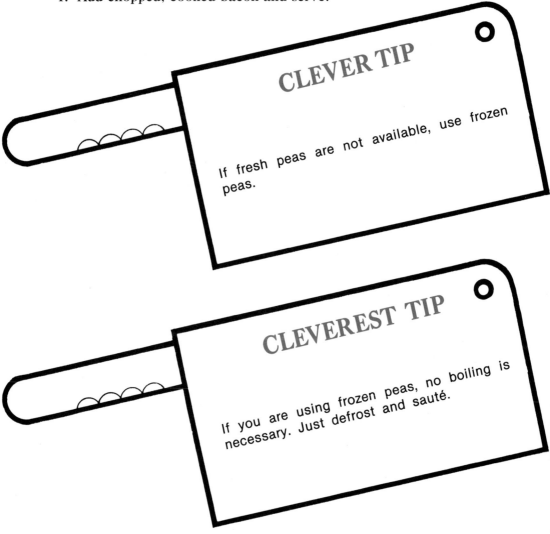

CLEVER TIP

If fresh peas are not available, use frozen peas.

CLEVEREST TIP

If you are using frozen peas, no boiling is necessary. Just defrost and sauté.

SEASONED BROCCOLI
2 portions

4 medium broccoli spears   *Salt and white pepper to taste*
1 tablespoon butter

1. Place broccoli spears in boiling salted water and cook just until they are al dente (approximately 4–5 minutes). DO NOT OVERCOOK.
2. Cool broccoli thoroughly under cold, running water. This stage can be done in advance.
3. Heat butter in a sauté pan until hot. DO NOT BURN.
4. Add blanched broccoli spears to sauté pan. Season with salt and white pepper to taste.
5. Turn occasionally and heat until hot. Serve.

Steve demonstrates the funky chicken.

BROILED TOMATO CROWN

1 medium tomato per person   *Grated Parmesan cheese*
Bread crumbs   *Melted butter*

1. Plane bottom of tomato to make a flat surface.
2. Cut top of tomato in a zigzag pattern to make a crown.
3. Combine bread crumbs with Parmesan cheese.
4. Put bread crumbs/Parmesan cheese mixture on cut top. Drizzle with melted butter.
5. Just prior to service, place under broiler until golden brown.

SAUTÉED ZUCCHINI
2 portions

1½ tablespoons butter   *2 small zucchini, thinly sliced*
2 cloves garlic, minced   *Salt and pepper to taste*

1. Heat butter in a sauté pan until hot. Do not burn butter.
2. Add minced garlic and heat for approximately 30 seconds.
3. Add sliced zucchini and toss to heat evenly.
4. Season with salt and pepper to taste.

SEASONED GREEN BEANS
2 portions

½ pound fresh green beans   *White pepper to taste*
1 tablespoon butter   *Salt to taste*

1. Rinse green beans under cold, running water. Cut off the ends and cut beans in half.
2. Place in boiling salted water and cook until al dente. DO NOT OVERCOOK. Cool immediately under cold, running water.
3. Melt the butter in a sauté pan.
4. Add blanched green beans and season with salt and white pepper. Heat and serve.

SAUTÉED ASPARAGUS TIPS

6 spears asparagus per person   Salt and white pepper
1 tablespoon butter

1. Rinse fresh asparagus under cold, running water. Cut stalks to leave approximately 3-inch pieces with the tips.
2. Keep 3-inch tips secured with a rubber band or butchers' twine. Place in boiling salted water and cook just until al dente. DO NOT OVERCOOK. Test by piercing asparagus with a fork. Fork should go in without much resistance.
3. Remove from pan and cool completely under cold, running water.
4. Remove fastener and carefully shake off excess water. Be careful not to break tips.
5. Melt the butter in a sauté pan and add the asparagus tips, salt, and white pepper.
6. Heat until hot and arrange on plates.

Dressed to kill and not even a nibble.

SAUTÉED CHINESE PEA PODS
2 portions

20 Chinese pea pods   *Salt and white pepper to taste*
Butter, as needed

1. Cut the very end of stem off pea pods.
2. Rinse pea pods under cold, running water. Pat dry.
3. Heat butter in a sauté pan. Add pea pods.
4. Season with salt and white pepper.
5. Heat until hot. Serve.

Everything we cook has to pass the Clever Cleaver S.E.E.
Test: Simple, Easy to prepare, and Elegant.

GONE
BANANAS!

BLARNEY BANANAS FLAMBÉ
2 portions

2 tablespoons butter
2 bananas, sliced
2 tablespoons sugar
¼ cup chopped walnuts
½ cup currants
Few dashes bitters

2 tablespoons Irish whiskey
½ cup Irish Cream (Baileys type)
Dash of cinnamon
Dash of nutmeg
Green crème de menthe (optional)
Ice cream

1. In a sauté pan, heat butter over medium heat.
2. Add sliced bananas and sprinkle with sugar. Flip bananas in pan to heat and to coat evenly with sugar.
3. Add walnuts, currants, and bitters. Combine.
4. *Pull pan away from heat* and CAREFULLY flambé with whiskey.
5. When flame goes out, add Irish Cream, cinnamon, and nutmeg. Heat.
6. In a dessert bowl, place a small amount of green crème de menthe. On that, place some ice cream. Top with Blarney Bananas Flambé. ENJOY!

CLEVER CREPES WITH FLAMING BANANAS

CHOCOLATE CREPE BATTER
10 crepes

2 medium eggs
1 cup half-and-half
½ cup flour
1½ teaspoons sugar

⅛ teaspoon salt
1 tablespoon cocoa powder for baking
Shaved chocolate for garnish

ORANGE CREPE BATTER
10 crepes

2 medium eggs
1 cup half-and-half
½ cup flour
1½ teaspoons sugar

⅛ teaspoon salt
1½ teaspoons chopped orange zest
Julienned orange zest for garnish

Zesting an orange.

STEP ONE: BATTER

1. In mixing bowl, using a wire whip, beat eggs and mix in the half-and-half.
2. Incorporate flour, sugar, and salt until smooth.
3. For chocolate crepes, add cocoa powder and mix thoroughly. Pass through a strainer to remove lumps. Proceed to cooking stage.
4. For orange crepes, pass the batter through a strainer to remove lumps and then add the orange zest. Proceed to cooking stage.

STEP TWO: CREPES

1. Heat 8-inch Teflon pan until hot.
2. Using a pastry brush or a paper towel, wipe bottom of pan with a thin coating of melted butter.
3. Using a 2-ounce ladle, place crepe batter in pan. Move pan to coat bottom evenly. Pour out excess batter.
4. When crepe begins to brown, turn over with rubber spatula. This will take approximately 10–15 seconds.
5. Cook on second side for 5–10 seconds.
6. Flip crepe out of pan onto an inverted plate to cool. Repeat process until batter is finished.
7. Let crepes cool. Cover and refrigerate until ready to use.

BANANA FILLING
2 portions

2 tablespoons butter	*Few dashes bitters*
3 large bananas, cut into ⅜-inch slices	*¼ cup Grand Marnier liqueur*
2 tablespoons sugar	*¾ cup whipping cream*
1 cup shelled walnuts	*Pinch of cinnamon*
½ cup currants	*Pinch of nutmeg*

STEP THREE: CREPE FILLING

1. Melt butter in large sauté pan and add sliced bananas. Coat bananas with melted butter.
2. Sprinkle bananas with sugar and flip to coat evenly.
3. Add walnuts, currants, and bitters. Combine.
4. *Pull pan away from flame* and CAREFULLY flambé with Grand Marnier.

5. When flame burns out, add whipping cream, cinnamon, and nutmeg. Mix and heat until whipping cream is reduced and slightly thickened.

STEP FOUR: CREPE ASSEMBLY

1. Place crepe on plate with the golden brown side on the plate.
2. Place Banana Filling on half of crepe. Fold the other half of crêpe over filling.
3. Top with a dollop of whipped cream. Sprinkle with either chocolate shavings or orange zest.

Putting the finishing touches on the crepes.

VALENTINE SWEETHEART

BAKED ALASKA
8 portions

1 angel food cake mix
17-ounce can dark sweet pitted
* cherries in heavy syrup*
Egg whites from 8 large eggs
¾ teaspoon cream of tartar
4 tablespoons powdered sugar

¼ cup Kirschwasser (cherry
* brandy)*
1 pint vanilla ice cream
1 tablespoon Kirschwasser, for top
* (optional)*

STEP ONE: CAKE PREPARATION

1. Mix angel food cake mix as per instructions on package.
2. Divide mix among four 7-inch heart-shaped cake pans.
3. Bake the cakes, cool, and remove from pans as per instructions on package.
4. Cut one cake in half crosswise to make it half its thickness.
5. Cut two other cakes, from the top-side down, about 1 inch inside the edge of the cake, following the contour of the heart shape. Save the inside piece from one of the cut cakes.
6. Hold cake pieces for assembly.
   NOTE: Cake pans do not have to be heart-shaped. Nor do they have to be exactly 7 inches.

STEP TWO: CHERRY PREPARATION

1. Drain can of cherries.
2. Cut cherries in half and hold for cake assembly.

STEP THREE: MERINGUE PREPARATION

1. Place egg whites in a clean, dry, stainless steel bowl.
2. Add cream of tartar and powdered sugar to egg whites.
3. Whip with electric mixer until whites form stiff peaks.
4. Begin cake assembly.

STEP FOUR: CAKE ASSEMBLY

1. Preheat oven to 500 degrees. Place thin layer of cake on an ovenproof platter and sprinkle with ¼ cup Kirschwasser.
2. On top of this piece of cake, stack two cake rings.
3. In cavity, place one layer of cherry halves.
4. Cut vanilla ice cream into slices and fill cavity to top of bottom cake ring.
5. On top of ice cream, place the center that was cut out of one of the cake rings.
6. Using a cake spatula, cover sides and top with a layer of meringue.
7. Place remainder of meringue in a pastry bag with a star tip. Pipe a line of meringue around bottom border of cake and around top border. Make a little heart in the middle of the top of the cake.
8. Place cake in the oven for approximately 1 minute, or just until it becomes golden brown. Remove from oven.
9. Cut a little cup out of meringue heart on top of cake. Fill with 1 tablespoon Kirschwasser and CAREFULLY light with match.
10. When flame goes out, cut cake and serve.
    NOTE: Step #9 is for showmanship and is optional.

FLAMING BANANAS BRISBANE
2 portions

2 slices pound cake
2 strawberries
1 tablespoon butter
1 tablespoon sugar
2 bananas
¼ cup raisins

½ cup chopped walnuts
Few dashes bitters
¼ cup Amaretto
1 cup whipping cream
Pinch of cinnamon
Pinch of nutmeg

1. Place a slice of pound cake on each of two plates.
2. Using a 1-inch-wide cookie cutter, cut a circle out of the center of each slice of cake.
3. Rinse each strawberry and pat dry. Cut the stems off and place flat-side down in the circle of each slice of cake.
4. In a sauté pan, heat the butter over medium heat.
5. Add the sugar and dissolve.
6. Peel bananas and cut in half lengthwise. Cut the long pieces in half to give 4 pieces for each banana.
7. Add banana pieces to pan. Heat and gently turn to heat other side.
8. Add the raisins, walnuts, and bitters. Combine and heat for 1 minute.
9. *Pull pan away from heat* and CAREFULLY flambé with Amaretto.
10. When flame subsides, add the whipping cream to the pan.
11. Carefully remove the banana pieces and place along the sides of the cake slices.
12. To the pan, add the cinnamon and nutmeg and let mixture thicken.
13. Spoon the mixture over the cake and bananas. ENJOY!

CLEVER TIP

If you prefer, this banana dessert is also excellent over vanilla ice cream instead of over cake.

STRAWBERRY FLAMBÉ
2 portions

2 tablespoons butter
2 cups hulled and sliced
  fresh strawberries
1½ tablespoons sugar
¼ cup currants
¼ cup chopped walnuts

Few dashes bitters
¼ cup Grand Marnier
½ cup whipping cream
Pinch each cinnamon and nutmeg
Vanilla ice cream

1. In a sauté pan, heat butter over medium heat.
2. Add sliced strawberries and sprinkle with sugar. Flip strawberries in pan to coat evenly with sugar. DO NOT OVERCOOK.
3. Add currants, walnuts, and bitters. Combine.
4. *Pull pan away from heat* and CAREFULLY flambé with Grand Marnier.
5. When flame goes out, add whipping cream, cinnamon, and nutmeg. Combine ingredients. Lower the heat and reduce to the correct consistency.
6. In a dessert bowl, place vanilla ice cream. Top with strawberry flambé. ENJOY!

CLEVER MARNIER ICE CREAM
4 portions

½ cup whipping cream   *1 pint your favorite ice cream*
Grand Marnier liqueur   *1 can lychee nuts*

1. Place the whipping cream in a clean, dry, stainless steel or glass bowl.
2. Add the Grand Marnier and whip until it forms stiff peaks.
3. Refrigerate for use.
   NOTE: Steps 1–3 can be done prior to dinner.
4. Scoop your favorite ice cream into serving bowls.
5. Place 3–4 lychee nuts around the ice cream in each bowl.
6. Top with a dollop of Grand Marnier whipped cream.
7. Enjoy with a cup of coffee.

Our first appearance on "Live with Regis & Kathie Lee" in March 1989. WABC-TV.

KAHLUA MOUSSE
4 servings

12 ounces semisweet chocolate
  (chips or block)
½ cup Kahlua (coffee liqueur)
½ cup whipping cream

2 tablespoons sugar
4 egg whites
Pinch of salt

1. Place the chocolate and the Kahlua in a stainless steel bowl and place this over a pan of simmering water (double boiler) until the chocolate melts. Stir occasionally.
2. When melted, remove the bowl from the heat and let cool.
3. In a clean, dry, stainless steel bowl, whip the whipping cream with sugar until stiff peaks form. Hold in the refrigerator.
4. In another clean, dry, stainless steel bowl, whip the egg whites with salt until stiff peaks form.
5. Fold the whipped egg whites into the whipped cream.
   NOTE: This step should be done when the chocolate is cooled.
6. Whip ⅓ of this egg white/whipped cream mixture into the chocolate.
7. Fold the remaining ⅔ of the egg white/whipped cream mixture into the chocolate, being careful not to overmix.
8. Place in individual serving bowls and refrigerate for at least 2 hours prior to service.

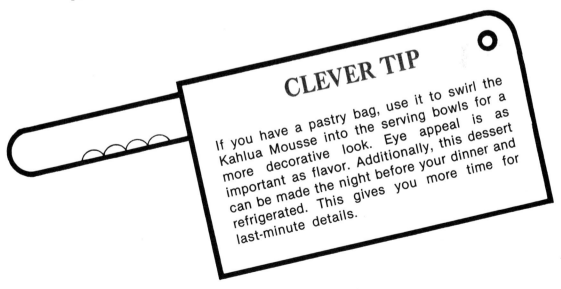

CLEVER TIP

If you have a pastry bag, use it to swirl the Kahlua Mousse into the serving bowls for a more decorative look. Eye appeal is as important as flavor. Additionally, this dessert can be made the night before your dinner and refrigerated. This gives you more time for last-minute details.

SAN DIEGO–STYLE CHEESECAKE
8-inch-by-8-inch-by-2-inch cheesecake

1 teaspoon lemon juice
8 ounces cream cheese
8 ounces ricotta cheese (1 cup)
1 cup sour cream
2 large eggs
4 tablespoons butter, melted and
  cooled

½ teaspoon vanilla
¾ cup sugar
1½ tablespoons flour
1½ tablespoons cornstarch
Your favorite jam (optional)

1. Preheat oven to 350 degrees. Place the lemon juice, cream cheese, ricotta cheese, sour cream, eggs, melted butter, and vanilla in a glass bowl.
2. Using an electric mixer, whip the ingredients. Start on slow speed to incorporate ingredients, then increase the speed.
3. In a separate bowl, use a fork to mix the sugar, flour, and cornstarch. Slowly add these to the other bowl, mixing with the electric mixer.
4. Pour into a lightly greased glass cake dish (8-inches-by-8-inches-by-2-inches). Shake pan to spread evenly.
5. Place in the center of the preheated oven.
6. Bake for 1 hour. Turn off the oven and leave cheesecake in the oven for an additional 2 hours.
7. Remove from the oven, cool, and refrigerate.
8. You can spread your favorite jam over the top of the cheesecake and serve out of the cake dish. Or, prior to spreading jam:
9. Run a knife around the outside of the cake. Carefully slide a spatula under all sides of the cake to loosen.
10. Turn cake out onto a cutting board.
11. Holding the cake firm with one hand, use a spatula to flip it over onto a serving platter.
12. Spread your favorite jam over the top. Cut, serve, and enjoy.

Backstage at the "Live with Regis & Kathie Lee" show—
WABC-TV.

EAT RIGHT, GET TIGHT

"THE CHOLESTEROL ZONE"

Worried about your cholesterol? Watch what you eat, exercise, and sing to the beat of "The Cholesterol Zone" with "The Clever Cleaver Brothers."

> You've just entered The Cholesterol Zone,
> Sure you're worried but you're not alone,
> Should you turn around and run?
> NO, join The Cleavers, have big fun.
> Don't feel lost or in despair,
> The Cleavers know – you have some fears.
> Over 200's the reading you got,
> "Lower that number," screamed your doc.
> Sit down, relax, and catch our show,
> We'll give you info you need to know.
> Avoid cholesterol and saturated fats,
> Good eating and exercise, you can do that.
> So settle back, make yourself at home,
> As we walk you through The Cholesterol Zone.

Nowadays, you can't turn on the television or pick up a newspaper or a magazine without hearing or reading something about cholesterol, sodium, and saturated fats, and the effect they have on us.

"The Clever Cleaver Brothers" agree that we should all be concerned with these issues, but they should not dominate our lives. We have always believed in creating recipes that were tasty and good-for-you, but we did not get carried away with specific health concerns. Since we began our business with the production of our "Cooking For Compliments" video cookbook, people have suggested that we produce videotapes on vegetarian cooking, as well as a myriad of other special-interest topics. Although all these topics have merit, we have always concentrated on topics with larger market appeal. Being "The People Chefs," we concentrate our efforts on what you, Mr. & Mrs. America, would be interested in most.

Because no two people are alike, and because everyone should fine-tune their diets to meet their own needs, we continue to present our recipes in their original simple, easy-to-prepare, and elegant form. However, we do have some very simple adjustments that can be made to all recipes to make them healthier. (This information is being offered from a culinary viewpoint, not as medical advice. Consult your physician should you have any concerns.) Consider some of these tips the next time you go shopping or step into the kitchen:

- Fresh fruit contains no cholesterol and is very low in fat. Eat as much as you like.
- Did you know that whole milk gets up to 49 percent of its calories from fat? Low-fat milk is better, but nonfat milk contains the least amount of fat.
- We know that omelets are very popular. But, did you know that egg yolks are very high in cholesterol and fat? Egg whites, on the other hand, contain no cholesterol and are high in protein. Egg whites can be substituted for whole eggs in most recipes.

Personally, when "The Clever Cleaver Brothers" make an omelet for ourselves, we make it using just egg whites and seasonings. However, we understand that most people want an omelet that is yellowish in color. Try making your next omelet using 1 whole egg and the whites from 2 or 3 large eggs. Whip the egg batter with 1 tablespoon nonfat milk, black pepper, and a few dashes of bitters.

This omelet looks the same as your traditional omelet, tastes great, and has less cholesterol and saturated fat. It is a very simple alteration with long-term advantages.

- Next time you make French toast, forget the yolks. Make your batter with egg whites, nonfat milk, cinnamon, nutmeg, and a couple of dashes of bitters. Just like the omelet, this new French toast looks the same as your usual French toast. It tastes great and contains no saturated fat from the egg yolks. Try it this way.
- As a rule of thumb, 2 egg whites are the equivalent of 1 large egg. For baking, substitute 3 egg whites for 2 whole eggs.
- We use margarine instead of butter, even for baking. When buying margarine, look for brands that list liquid oil as the first ingredient.
- Cheese is delicious on crackers, in an omelet, with fresh fruit, and in many other recipes. However, cheese is very high in butterfat content. When selecting a cheese, try a cheese that is marked "low-fat" or "skim-milk." For our omelets, we use farmers cheese. It's good for you and delicious.
- A lot of lunches consist of hard-boiled eggs, potato chips, soft drinks, and a sandwich that is bulked up with fatty meats, hard cheese, and lots of mayonnaise.

- Many processed meats such as sausage, bologna, salami, and hot dogs are up to 80 percent fat. Read the labels and look for products that say "reduced fat." They should be no more than 10 percent fat by weight.
- Most mayonnaise is made with egg yolks and whole eggs. It is high in fat, cholesterol, and calories. Instead of mayonnaise, use some Dijon mustard on your sandwich. Complete your sandwich with some crisp lettuce, alfalfa sprouts, tomato slices, and whole wheat bread.
- When choosing an oil, corn oil, safflower oil, and sunflower oil are low in saturated fats. Even better for you are olive oil and canola oil. "The Clever Cleaver Brothers" use olive oil in a lot of recipes. It is good for us and it tastes great.
- Speaking of oils, lunch, and saturated fats, many salad dressings are high in calories, fat, and cholesterol. Next time you are having a salad, try making a delicious, good-for-you dressing with the following ingredients: 1 part olive oil, 2 parts rice wine vinegar, chopped tarragon, Dijon mustard, black pepper, and some low-sodium Worcestershire sauce.
- The best way to enjoy salad is by sprinkling it with flavored vinegars and black pepper.
- When preparing chicken, remove the skin and trim the fat. Rub a little bitters on the chicken to give it the golden brown color that we usually see when the skin crisps. Season the chicken with fresh fruit juices – such as lemon, lime, or orange – and herbs. The herbs can be fresh or dehydrated. Try tarragon or basil. Prepare your chicken on the BBQ grill or in the oven.
- When selecting meat, look for lean cuts such as flank steak or sirloin. Trim excess fat. When roasting meat, roast on a rack so the fat will drip away. When browning meats, such as for stew, pour off the excess fat before continuing with the recipe. If you are going to BBQ a steak, trim the fat and marinate with low-sodium Worcestershire sauce, black pepper, and garlic powder.
- When preparing vegetables, steam them until they are al dente (crisp to the bite), so they retain their color and nutrients. If you want a sauce for your vegetables, make one with melted margarine and a few dashes of bitters.
- Baked potatoes are good for us. However, all the ingredients that we usually pile on the potato are not so good for us. On your next baked potato try topping it with plain nonfat yogurt and some chopped chives.
- Pasta topped with cream sauces is not the best way to go. Next time you make pasta, try topping it with a marinara sauce made from fresh plum tomatoes.

Not only are we barraged with news reports on cholesterol and saturated fats, but take a walk in the grocery store and look at the products on the shelves. Every other manufacturer has some claim on their packages boasting about their product being good for us. They are either "low-fat," "low-cholesterol," or something in between. Although their claims may be true and may sound good, careful investigation and a little common sense might reveal that, in reality, their products may not be all that good for us. Careful ingredient analysis and comparing "apples to apples" is the name of the game.

Next time you go to the supermarket, think about these ideas:

- Although we have all heard this a hundred times, as simple as it sounds, don't go shopping when you are hungry. When hungry, everything looks good and we are in a hurry to buy the food, go home, and eat. At times like this we usually buy junk food.
- Don't shop when you are in a hurry. Give yourself adequate time to read the labels and compare ingredient statements. Additionally, the nutritional analysis will tell you how many calories per serving, the amount of sodium, fats, etc., per serving.
- Speaking of labels, as we mentioned above, a lot of labels have healthful buzz words to grab your attention. But beware. A lot of food products that say "contains no cholesterol" on the label may not contain cholesterol themselves, but instead contain a high amount of saturated fat, which contributes to cholesterol in the body. For example, take peanut butter. Although it may say "no cholesterol" on the label, the nutritional analysis indicates that approximately three-fourths of its calories come from fat. Fat contributes to high cholesterol.
- It's almost ridiculous that some foods say "no cholesterol" on the label and people think the products are healthy. Although we love items such as potato chips, ourselves, we don't deceive ourselves into thinking they are healthful. Reading the ingredient statement and the nutritional analysis reveals that even one ounce of the chips contains a high amount of fat.
- Sodium is another culprit. By simply reading the ingredient analysis we can see how much sodium per serving size an item contains.
- Just a simple glance at the ingredient list on a product may tell us everything we need to know about that product. Ingredients are listed in descending order. The closer it is listed to the beginning of the ingredient statement, the more of that item the product contains. For example, a container of chicken stock base that we picked up lists the

ingredients as follows: salt, sugar, chicken fat, monosodium glutamate, soybean oil. . . . In this case, salt is the major ingredient, followed by sugar, with the only mention of chicken being the chicken fat which doesn't appear until the third ingredient. Because of labeling laws, this product could not be called chicken base. They call it soup base – chicken flavor. It does taste like chicken once you get past the salt.

- Salt deserves a little more attention. Be aware that it may be listed as sodium in the ingredient listing. If something is listed as "sodium-free," that means it has less than 5 milligrams of sodium per serving. "Very low-sodium" means it has less than 35 milligrams of sodium per serving. "Low-sodium" means it has 140 milligrams or less of sodium per serving. "Reduced-sodium" means the product was processed to reduce the usual sodium level by 75 percent. If something is labeled "unsalted," "no salt added," or "without added salt," that means that it is made without the salt that is normally used, but the product still contains the salt that is naturally in the food.

- Even "healthy" items such as bran muffins can be deceiving. A lot of companies use the overblown perception that oat bran lowers cholesterol to sell their products. However, if you look closely at the nutrition statement, you may see that they are high in calories and high in fat. We are not saying that oat bran muffins are not good for you; we are just suggesting that you analyze the ingredients and make an intelligent purchase.

- If we compared a lot of food items, we would see that we have all had some misconceptions regarding their nutritional comparison. For example, we all know that bacon is high in fat. But, did you know that if we compared certain cookies to the same number of cooked bacon strips we would find that the cookies have more fat than the bacon? Certainly, bacon and cookies are just an example. There are many other foods that would surprise us.

- With other foods that we may be accustomed to eating, by making some very minor changes, we can eat virtually the same foods but in a much healthier fashion. For example, a 3-ounce portion of tuna packed in water may have as little as 1.0 gram of fat. But take the same portion of tuna that is packed in vegetable oil and it could have more than 17 grams of fat. Who needs the oil and the fat? Not "The Clever Cleaver Brothers."

- Don't be misled by food groups that sound healthy; they may not all be. For example, plain nonfat yogurt is very low in fat and is a healthy product. Take whole-milk yogurt that has fruit in it and the calorie and fat contents multiply.

- We've mentioned a few times that we should always compare "apples to apples." Let's keep that in mind whenever we compare ingredient statements, nutritional analyses of products, and calorie content. Most products list these by "serving." Comparing, for example, some "lite" and "low-salt" sauces, as we mentioned earlier in our Introduction, we find that, adjusted for amount per "serving size," ANGOSTURA low-sodium soy sauce contains a fraction of the amount of sodium as other "lite" products. Again, be sure to compare "apples to apples," and shop wisely!

A night out with the girls.

FOOD, POTS and PANS, and KNOW-HOW

CULINARY TERMS AND TERMINOLOGY

AGAINST THE GRAIN – refers to cutting a piece of meat in the opposite direction than the connective tissue is going. This will help to make the meat more tender.

AGING – describes the process of tenderizing a piece of meat at a controlled temperature for a particular length of time so that the natural enzymes will break down the connective tissue.

AL DENTE – refers to cooking something until it is firm or even crisp to the bite – NOT OVERCOOKING it until it becomes soft.

BASTING – keeping a food item moist as it cooks by coating it with its own drippings or with some stock.

BIND – causing food items to adhere to one another, sometimes by using an egg yolk.

BOUQUET GARNI – used most often in a court bouillon, a bouquet garni is made of parsley, thyme, bay leaves, and peppercorns that have been tied in a bundle, either in cheesecloth or between two pieces of celery stalk. If celery is used, the curves should sit inside each other with the herbs and seasonings between the stalks. Then, tie the celery stalks together with butchers' twine.

CARAMELIZE – heating sugar or foods containing sugar, causing it to brown and providing a distinctive flavor.

COLLAGEN – the white connective tissue in meat.

COMPOUND BUTTER – butter with any ingredients added to it to give it a particular taste or flavor. Not only does it enhance the flavor of a piece of meat or fish very nicely, it also acts as the perfect natural garnish. Soften butter in a mixing bowl and incorporate complementing ingredients. Spoon down the center of a piece of plastic wrap and roll it to form a cylinder tube. Twist the ends and place in your freezer. Remove from freezer approximately 20 minutes prior to use so it will temper. Cut thin slices of the compound butter and put on top of your hot meat or fish. Return the remainder to the freezer for future use. For maximum flavor, compound butters should be used within 4 weeks.

COURT BOUILLON – a seasoned liquid in which a food item is poached. It is made by adding cut celery, cut carrots, white wine, lemon juice, and a bouquet garni to water and simmering the mixture for 30–45 minutes. The liquid is then strained and used to poach a piece of fish or other food item. While poaching, the water should *never* come to a boil or it will cause the food to break apart.

CROUTONS – bread cut into cubes and then fried, broiled, or baked in butter and seasonings. Smaller croutons are used on salads. Larger, different-shaped croutons are used as an underliner on the plate for meat items such as medallions of pork tenderloin.

DEGLAZING – using any liquid to extract the natural essence of ingredients from the bottom of a roasting pan or a sauté pan so that the drippings can be incorporated into the sauce. Although, technically, any liquid can be used, a liquid other than water is best so that it will enhance the flavor of the sauce rather than dilute it. Wine and stock are two good choices.

DOLLOP – such as a dollop of whipped cream; using a spoon to plop an amount of an ingredient on top of something, keeping its natural appearance.

DREDGING – the act of lightly coating a food item with seasoned flour. Do this just prior to cooking so that the food item will not become soggy.

DUSTING – the process of lightly sprinkling a worktable, cutting board, or greased cake pan with plain flour to prevent dough from sticking. If a recipe calls for dusting a food item with flour or sugar, etc., this refers to a *very light* coating.

ELASTIN – the yellow connective tissue in meat.

FLORENTINE – a preparation using cooked spinach as a bed on which other ingredients are placed.

FOLD – usually refers to combining ingredients with an item that has had air whipped into it. An example would be adding items to whipped cream. This is done by bringing your utensil down into the whipped cream with a vertical motion and bringing the utensil back up the other side of the bowl while turning it over the top of the whipped cream to fold in the ingredients. Using this method, no air is lost.

FORCEMEAT – refers to a stuffing made of chopped meats and seasonings.

GARNISH – refers to enhancing the appearance of a plate or food item with the addition of a decorative item. Garnishes should always be edible.

GRATED GINGER – Many recipes call for ground ginger, others call for fresh, minced ginger. In most of our recipes, we use freshly grated ginger. Trim the outside skin, or the bark as we refer to it, off the portion of the fresh ginger to be used. Run it along the finer section of a vegetable grater. The ginger "pulp" comes through the grater and the stringy portion stays behind. Use the "pulp" in your recipe. This is what we mean by "grated ginger."

HORS D'OEUVRES – small appetizers served as the first course. Many times the hors d'oeuvres will be enjoyed with cocktails before the meal is served.

INCORPORATE – to mix items together.

JULIENNE – refers to cutting food – usually vegetables – in thin, match-like strips.

LIAISON – used to bind sauces and usually made of egg yolks and cream.

MARINATING – placing an item such as a piece of meat into a liquid made of vinegar or fruit juices, oil, and seasonings for the purpose of tenderizing it and enhancing the flavor.

MIREPOIX – pronounced *mere-eh-pwah*, this is a rough-cut (or peasant-cut, as it is sometimes called) of onions, celery, and carrots used to add flavor to soup and sauce stocks, soups, sauces, and roasted meats.

NAPÉ – when you lace something lightly with sauce, you give it a napé of sauce.

PAPILLOTE – pronounced *pah-pee-oht*, this refers to cooking an item in parchment paper to seal in flavors and juices.

PIQUANT – describes the pungent taste of a sauce, salad dressing, or other food item.

PLANE – cutting a flat surface, such as on the bottom of a food item, so that it will sit flat on a plate.

REDUCE – reducing the quantity of stock or a sauce by simmering it, thus giving it a richer flavor and consistency.

ROUX – pronounced *roo*, this is made of 50 percent fat and 50 percent flour by weight and is used to thicken sauces. The three types of roux are white, blond, and brown. The darker roux should be used to thicken darker sauces. Not only does the roux become darker as it is heated, it becomes stronger as the gluten strands in the flour develop. This is called "energizing the roux." A roux can be heated on the stove, in a saucepan, or sauté pan, or it can be cooked in the oven in a roasting pan. Whatever the cooking method, cook the roux slowly so it does not burn. While cooking, mix periodically with a wooden spoon.

SEASONED FLOUR – flour with salt and pepper added to it for the purpose of dredging a food item. If the food being dredged is very light, white pepper is sometimes used instead of black pepper.

TEMPER – to alter the temperature of something.

TOURNÉE – refers to the decorative cut of a vegetable to resemble the shape of a football. Most often done with carrots and potatoes.

TRANSLUCENT – describes the clear appearance of certain food items after cooking, such as onion.

ZEST – a thin strip of lemon or orange peel used for flavoring.

INGREDIENTS

BUTTER

Basically, butter is the fat of cream that has been separated from other milk components by means of agitation. Butter can be made from either sweet or sour cream.

Butter is composed of approximately 80 percent butterfat, 16 percent water, 2 percent protein, and 2 percent salt and minerals. Salted butter has better keeping qualities and is generally the preferred butter. Salted butter could be *demi-sel,* with a salt content of 3–5 percent, or it could be *salted,* with a salt content of 8–10 percent.

Butter is largely graded according to its flavor, but also taken into consideration is color, body, and salt content. A good butter should have a semisoft consistency at room temperature and should not sweat. If the butter does sweat, this is an indicator that it contains too much water.

COMPOUND BUTTER – butter with any ingredients added to it to give it a particular taste or flavor. Not only does it enhance the flavor of a piece of meat or fish very nicely, but it also acts as the perfect natural garnish.

CLARIFIED BUTTER – the butterfat that remains after removal of the salt and milk solids from butter. We do this because it is the milk solids that will brown and burn when heated to a high temperature. Using clarified butter allows us to sauté at high temperatures without smoking or burning.

The simplest method for clarifying butter is to melt it over low heat, letting the milk solids and salt settle to the bottom of the pan. Skim or pour off the butter fat and discard the residue.

BEURRE NOISETTE – also known as brown butter or hazelnut butter – butter heated just to the point where it begins to turn brown and give off a hazelnut aroma. When sautéing certain items, beurre noisette is used because it adds color and flavor.

BEURRE NOIR – also known as black butter–essentially beurre noisette that has been further heated to a darker color.

COOKING OILS

Fats fall into three categories: saturated, polyunsaturated, and monounsaturated. Saturated fats are the least healthy, tending to increase the level of cholesterol in the blood. Monounsaturated fats are neutral because they do not tend to raise or lower cholesterol levels significantly. Polyunsaturated fats tend to lower the cholesterol level. Therefore, it is probably advisable to use polyunsaturated fats.

Vegetable oils seem to contain fewer saturated fats than animal oils. Corn and soybean oil work the best for deep-fat frying. Olive oil and shortening seem to work the best for normal frying and baking.

Based on the amount of saturated fats they contain, the following is a list of fats, in our order of preference, starting with canola oil, which is the most healthy, and going to coconut oil, which is the least healthy.

1. Canola oil
2. Safflower oil
3. Sunflower oil
4. Corn oil
5. Olive oil
6. Soybean oil
7. Peanut oil
8. Cottonseed oil
9. Lard
10. Palm oil
11. Butterfat
12. Coconut oil

OLIVE OIL

After olives are picked or "combed" from the olive trees, the olives are sorted and taken to a crusher, where they are rolled into a paste. The paste is spread on nylon discs and the discs are locked into a hydraulic press that forces the liquid out. A centrifugal drum separates a dark liquid from the greenish-gold oil.

Variations in olive oils are caused by the type of tree and the country of origin. This could dictate color, flavor, and aroma.

After pressing, impurities and excess oleic acid are removed by refining. The product that is left is called "pure olive oil." "Virgin" olive oil has not been refined and contains no more than 3.3 percent oleic acid. "Extra Virgin" contains no more than 1 percent oleic acid. Small amounts of the virgin or extra virgin oil are added to pure olive oil to enhance its flavor.

HERBS AND SPICES

ALLSPICE –the dried berry of a West Indian tree of the myrtle family, with a flavor resemling a blend of cinnamon, nutmeg, and cloves.

ANISE – dried aromatic seed with a subtle licorice flavor. Used to flavor both foods and medicines.

BASIL – also know as sweet basil, a plant of the mint family. It is grown in both Europe and the United States, and is a common ingredient in French and Italian dishes.

BAY LEAVES – dried leaves of the edible European laurel. Available whole or ground.

CAPERS – from a shrub of the Mediterranean region, these greenish pods or young berries are pickled for use as a seasoning.

CARAWAY SEED – dried aromatic seed with cuminlike flavor, used in both foods and medicines.

CARDAMOM – fruit of an East Indian herb of the ginger family, whose fairly sweet seeds flavor both foods and medicine.

CAYENNE – ground blend of the most potent chili peppers.

CELERY FLAKES – dehydrated garden celery, a European herb of the carrot family.

CELERY SEED – a pungent seed of wild celery, of different origin from that of celery flakes.

CHERVIL – delicate and mild-flavored herb, parsleylike in flavor.

CHILI POWDER – chili peppers ground to a powder and blended with other seasonings – cumin, oregano, garlic, among others.

CHIVE – a perennial plant of the onion family, whose long tubular leaves have a mild flavor.

CILANTRO – sometimes called Mexican parsley. Its distinct flavor is used widely in Mexican dishes.

CINNAMON – bark from any of various trees of the laurel family. Used in stick or ground form.

CLOVES – tiny, dried unopened flower buds from a tree of the myrtle family. Used whole or ground.

CUMIN – a plant of the carrot family from southern Asia, bearing aromatic, somewhat bitter seeds. An ingredient in curry and chili powder.

CURRY POWDER – a mixture of several ground spices from India – among them cayenne, coriander, cumin, turmeric.

DILL SEED – dried fruit of the dill plant. Widely used to flavor pickles.

DILL WEED – dried leaves of a European herb of the carrot family. Grown in both Europe and the United States, used widely in Middle Eastern cuisine.

FENNEL – aromatic seed from European herb of the carrot family, with a taste that hints of anise.

FILÉ – also known as Gumbo Filé, a powder made from young, tender sassafras leaves. It flavors and thickens, and is essential in Creole dishes.

GARLIC – potent bulbous herb of the lily family. A favorite of "The Clever Cleaver Brothers."

GINGER – spice ground from the pungent root of a tropical Oriental plant. Or grated fresh from the market.

HORSERADISH – a large-leafed perennial herb of the mustard family. Its roots are ground or grated to make a condiment.

JUNIPER BERRIES – dried berries of an evergreen shrub of the pine family.

MACE – whole or ground East Indian spice from the dried covering of the nutmeg, and milder.

MARJORAM – dried leaves derived from plants of the mint family, with quite a strong flavor. To be used sparingly.

MINT – leaves or flakes, from a family of aromatic plants.

MUSTARD SEED – seed of one of several plants of the mustard family, grown in Europe and North America.

NUTMEG – aromatic ground seed of the nutmeg tree.

OREGANO – also called wild marjoram, these aromatic leaves are widely used in Italian dishes.

PAPRIKA – ground pods of sweet red pepper, used for flavor and color.

PARSLEY – herb of the carrot family native to southern Europe. Used fresh or dried as a seasoning or garnish.

PEPPER (BLACK) – dried small, immature berries of a tropical climbing vine.

PEPPER (WHITE) – mature hulled berries of a tropical climbing vine, milder than black pepper.

PEPPERCORN – whole dried black pepper berry.

PICKLING SPICE – blend of whole spices such as mustard seed, bay leaves, red pepper, allspice, and ginger, used in pickling and preserving.

PIMIENTO – ripe, fleshy fruit of European sweet pepper, used as a brightly colored garnish or as a stuffing for olives.

POPPY SEED – tiny fragrant black seed of the poppy plant. A native of Holland.

POULTRY SEASONING – mixture of fragrant herbs – marjoram, savory, thyme – and sage. Used primarily in poultry and fish stuffings.

PUMPKIN PIE SPICE – blend of spices – usually cinnamon, nutmeg, ginger, cloves – used to flavor pumpkin, as well as other fruits and vegetable dishes.

RED PEPPER – whole, ground, or crushed pods of hot red chili peppers. Milder than cayenne.

ROSEMARY – dry, needlelike leaves from a shrub of the mint family.

SAFFRON – dried stigmas of a purple-flowered crocus. Its orange powder was used at one time as a dye.

SAGE – grayish green dried leaf of a shrub of the mint family, with a strong, somewhat bitter flavor.

SAVORY – of summer and winter savories, summer savory is the more delicate and versatile, often used to enhance vegetables.

SESAME SEEDS – seeds hulled from pods of an East Indian herb, with nutlike flavor.

SHALLOT – member of the onion family, producing small, clustered bulbs like those of garlic. And, just like garlic, a "Clever Cleaver Brothers" favorite.

SORREL – a plant with sour juice, sometimes called "sourgrass," whose long, slender leaves are used fresh.

SOY SAUCE – a liquid extracted from soy beans fermented and cured. Used primarily in Chinese and Japanese dishes.

TARRAGON – aromatic leaves with aniselike flavor. A principal ingredient in Bernaise sauce, it is used also in pickles and in vinegar.

THYME – aromatic leaves of a plant in the mint family, used widely in lamb dishes, stuffings, fish dishes, and good French cuisine.

TURMERIC – root of an East Indian herb of the ginger family. Bright yellow in color, it has a mustardlike flavor. An ingredient in curry.

COMPLEMENTING SEASONINGS

BEEF: bay leaves, chives, cloves, cumin, garlic, pepper, marjoram, rosemary, and savory.

BREAD: caraway, marjoram, oregano, poppy seed, rosemary, and thyme.

FISH: chervil, dill, fennel, tarragon, garlic, parsley, and thyme.

FRUIT: anise, cinnamon, coriander, cloves, ginger, and mint.

LAMB: garlic, marjoram, oregano, rosemary, and thyme.

PORK: coriander, cumin, garlic, ginger, pepper, sage, savory, and thyme.

POULTRY: garlic, oregano, rosemary, savory, and sage.

SALADS: basil, chives, tarragon, garlic, parsley, and sorrel.

SOUPS: bay leaves, chervil, tarragon, marjoram, parsley, savory, and rosemary.

VEGETABLES: basil, chervil, chives, dill, tarragon, marjoram, mint, parsley, pepper, and thyme.

KNIVES AND KITCHEN TOOLS

KNIVES

Next to a chef's hands, we believe the most important and usually the most often used tools in the kitchen are a set of knives. If you have ever been a little overwhelmed by the many different brands and types of knives on the market, you are surely not alone. Just like automobiles, knives are available from the very cheap models all the way to the expensive, high-quality brands. In between, there are some very good quality knives at reasonable prices. Although we will not recommend a particular brand, we will pass along some points to consider.

When viewing knives, you will see the type with plastic handles. These were developed for durability and also so that the knives could be passed through the dishwasher without harm to the handle. Because we know that you will handle your knife with the respect it deserves, and because a knife *should never be put in the dishwasher,* we recommend always buying knives with wooden handles. Plastic looks as cheap as it is. We also suggest buying knives that have the blades running all the way to the ends of the handles. Some knives have blades that only go part way through the handle; these are not the best quality.

The blades of knives are made of either stainless steel or carbon steel. Stainless steel is harder to keep sharp than carbon steel, but easier to keep shiny. Although carbon steel knives may not look as bright as stainless steel, a high-carbon steel knife is easier to sharpen and holds a sharp edge longer. Professionally speaking, I would recommend carbon steel knives. However, if you bought stainless steel knives you would still be getting a good product. Either way, go with wooden handles and make sure the blade runs all the way through the handle.

Most cuts/injuries are due to a dull knife because the user has to push and press too hard. After buying a good knife, keep it sharp by occasionally using a sharpening stone and by very frequently honing the knife on a steel.

After using your knife, keep it clean by washing it with soapy water. Use a scouring pad on the carbon blade, if necessary. Rinse and dry the knife and rub a little salad oil on the blade to keep it from tarnishing. Never let the knife soak in the sink. Not only is this very dangerous for someone reaching into the sink, but it will also damage the wooden handle. Knives should be kept in a knife rack or a knife block. Throwing them into a drawer could damage the blades.

Now that you know how to choose and care for your knives, let us describe the ones we keep in our kitchen:

BONING KNIFE – has a very thin, pointed blade and is used for getting very close to the bone while cutting away raw meat. Boning knives come with both stiff and flexible blades. They also come in different sizes. We use one with a 5-inch flexible blade.

BUTCHER KNIFE – has a heavy, curved, and pointed blade and is used to section meat. It is generally not necessary for the home kitchen.

CLAM KNIFE – is similar in size to the paring knife and has a flat, thin, sharp blade. It is used to open fresh clams.

CLEAVER – no, not "Clever Cleaver." We're talking about the knife. It has a heavy, square blade and is most often associated with Chinese cooking. Certainly not a necessity, but a good tool in the kitchen.

FORK – although not a knife, a heavy-duty fork is a must. This is used to turn roasts in the oven and hold the roast during slicing.

FRENCH KNIFE – this knife is used most often and it comes in different sizes. Choose the one that feels most comfortable in your hand. We use a 10-inch knife but many people prefer the smaller 8-inch version.

OYSTER KNIFE – knife with a thicker blade than the clam knife, and the end curves slightly. It is used to open fresh oysters.

PARING KNIFE – has a very short, pointed blade and is generally used for decorative work. It is very useful in the kitchen.

SLICER – this knife has a long, narrow blade and is used for slicing roasts. It usually has a rounded or a flat edge and the most common sizes are 12-inch and 14-inch blades. We use the 12-inch version.

STEEL – definitely needed to help maintain a sharp edge on your knives.

KITCHEN TOOLS

BAKING PAN – similar to a roasting pan and used for baked goods, usually without a cover.

CHINA CAP – a heavy-duty pointed strainer with holes much larger than a sieve. They come in different sizes, and are generally used for straining.

COLANDER – looks like a stainless steel bowl with many holes. It has handles and has a base under the bottom to keep it elevated. Different sizes are available. It is used for draining foods.

DOUBLE BOILER – one pan sets on top of the other. Water is placed in the bottom pan and brought to a boil with the food being heated in the top pan. They come in different sizes.

FOOD MILL – used to purée vegetables for cream soups and other uses.

GRATER – used to grate cheese and vegetables.

LADLES – metal bowls of varying capacities attached to metal handles. The capacity is usually stamped on the handle in ounces.

MEASURING CUPS – set usually consists of 1-cup measure, ¾ cup, ⅔ cup, ½ cup, ⅓ cup, ¼ cup, and ⅛ cup.

MEASURING SPOONS – set usually consists of 1 tablespoon, ½ tablespoon, 1 teaspoon, ½ teaspoon, ¼ teaspon, and ⅛ teaspoon.

PARISIENNE SCOOP – or melon baller as it is often called, usually has two different-sized scoops on either side of a short handle, and is used to scoop balls of melon and potatoes.

PASTRY BAGS – or piping bags as they are often called, come in various sizes with several decorative tips available. Used to decorate cakes and for additional decorative purposes.

PASTRY BRUSH – not necessary, but a good addition to an equipment package. Most often used to apply melted butter or an egg-wash to baked items.

ROASTING PAN – rectangular pans with covers. These pans come in different sizes and are used for roasting meats and other foods in the oven.

SAUCEPAN – comes in many sizes and with covers. This type of pan is often used and is a must in the kitchen.

SAUTÉ PAN – often called a frying pan, this pan is round with a sloping side and comes in many different sizes. Like the saucepans, these are a must in every kitchen.

SHEET PAN – rectangular pans with very low sides used for baking cookies and other foods. They come in different sizes.

SIEVE – fine mesh supported by a round frame with a handle. This is used for straining foods and sauces and comes in different sizes.

SPATULAS – equip your kitchen with a good stainless steel spatula and a wooden spatula.

SPOONS – there are many types and sizes on the market made of various materials. Every kitchen should be equipped with at least one solid spoon and one slotted spoon, each approximately 12 inches in length. We recommend the stainless steel version. Additionally, invest in a couple of wooden spoons to use in pans where you are concerned about protecting the finish (such as the Teflon type).

STOCKPOT – large pot with high side, usually used for making stocks and soups. They have handles and covers and come in many different sizes. Buy the size that is most practical for the intended use(s).

TONGS – we recommend leaving the "hot dog tongs" with the loop handles at the grocery store. Instead, invest in the stainless steel type with the spring action.

WHIPS – wire whips come in all sizes, from the tiny ones of approximately 5 inches to the large commercial versions that are over 3 feet in length and used in huge kettles. We recommend a couple of the very smallest wire whips for use in small saucepans and in very small mixing bowls. We also recommend a heavier-gauge wire whip approximately 12 inches in length.

We recommend the all-stainless steel versions. Avoid the ones with wooden handles. Wood will not hold up as long as stainless steel if it is left soaking in the sink, and the stainless steel looks more professional. This is more personal taste than anything else.

ZESTER – used for extracting the zest from oranges and lemons.

METHODS OF COOKING

BAKING – refers to cooking by dry heat, most often done in an oven. Most home ovens are conventional ovens but some newer models are available with a fan which circulates the hot air and provides faster cooking times and more even cooking. These ovens are most commonly referred to as convection ovens.

The term baking is usually associated with the cooking of doughs and batters for breads, cakes, cookies, etc. When this dry method of cooking in an oven is used on meat items, it is usually referred to as ROASTING.

BLANCHING – refers to partially cooking a food product, stopping the cooking process, and finishing the cooking at the time of use. Technically, blanching can be accomplished by using any method of cooking, but it is most often associated with cooking vegetables in boiling, salted water until they are al dente (crisp to the bite). Then, quickly, the vegetables are cooled completely under cold, running water to stop the cooking process. At the time of service, the vegetables could then be quickly sautéed to heat thoroughly and finish cooking.

BOILING – refers to cooking in a liquid that is at a temperature of 212 degrees Fahrenheit or 100 degrees centigrade.

BRAISING – refers to cooking a food product in a small quantity of liquid in a covered pan. This is most often done with meat items. Some meats, such as Swiss steaks, which are dredged in seasoned flour, are browned first, and then braised.

BROILING – refers to cooking under or over direct heat. We usually broil in the oven at home and broil over the heat on the char-broiler (barbecue).

FLAMBÉING – adding a liqueur to a dish causing it to flame until the alcohol burns off. The residual flavor enhances the dish nicely.

FRYING – refers to cooking food in hot fat that is usually 350–375 degrees. When food is completely submerged in hot fat, this is called deep-fat frying. If a food item is cooked in a small amount of fat in a frying pan, this is called **PAN FRYING**.

GRILLING – refers to cooking food on a heated flat surface.

PAN BROILING – refers to cooking food – usually a meat item with a sufficient amount of fat to prevent sticking – in a dry, very hot frying pan. The fat is poured out of the pan as the meat cooks.

PARBOILING – refers to the method of partially cooking food by boiling, as described in detail in the BLANCHING section.

POACHING – refers to cooking a tender food item by simmering it in a seasoned liquid. Salmon is an example of an item that is sometimes poached. The seasoned liquid is called a court bouillon and is made by adding cut celery and carrots, white wine, lemon juice, and a bouquet garni to water, and simmering it for 30–45 minutes. The liquid is strained and then used for poaching. While poaching, the water should *never* come to a boil or it will cause the food item to break apart.

(See description of bouquet garni in "Culinary Terms and Terminology.")

ROASTING – described in the BAKING section.

SAUTÉING – the word sauté actually means "to jump." Food is cooked in a sauté pan in a *very small amount of fat* and on *high heat.* The food is cooked very quickly.

SEARING – refers to browning the surface of meat quickly on high heat. This seals in the natural juices.

SIMMERING – refers to cooking in a liquid between 185 and 195 degrees Fahrenheit.

STEAMING – refers to cooking food by exposing it to steam. This can be done by placing food such as vegetables in a strainer over boiling water.

STEEPING – refers to soaking an item in a liquid just below the boiling point to extract flavor or color. Tea bags are steeped in water.

STEWING – see entry on BRAISING.

STIR-FRYING – refers to a method of cooking similar to sautéing, but most often associated with the Chinese method of cooking in a wok.

MEASURES

When reference is made to how many ounces are in a particular measure, it is always referring to liquid ounces. For example, a pint has 16 liquid ounces. A good way to remember this equivalency is: a pint is a pound the world around.

Other measures include:

CUP (8 ounces)
PINT (16 ounces)
QUART (32 ounces)
HALF-GALLON (64 ounces)
GALLON (128 ounces)

CUTS AND SIZES

Often, recipes will make reference to a term that dictates the shape and/or size of a particular cut. Listed are some often-referred-to terms:

ALLUMETTE – shoestring cut

BRUNOISE – (pronounced brun-whaz) fine dice approximately ⅛ inch

JULIENNE – matchlike cut approximately 1 inch long

PEARL – small, round shape

PEASANT – refers to a rough cut

TOURNÉE – a cut resembling the shape of a football

CONVERSIONS

RECIPE CONVERSION

All recipes provide a yield, or the amount that they will produce. Many times we require either a smaller yield or perhaps a greater yield than the recipe calls for. Here is how to convert any given recipe to produce the amount that you desire:

Divide the number of servings that you require by the number of servings given in the recipe. Then, multiply each ingredient by your answer. This will tell you how much of each ingredient to use, in order to give you the required number of servings.

For example, if a given recipe yields 4 servings and you only wanted to make enough for 2 people, you would divide 2 (required number of servings) by 4 (number of servings given in the recipe) and get a multiplier of .50, or one half. Multiply each ingredient by one-half to give you the correct amounts in order to yield a recipe for 2 portions.

Now, if for example you had to increase the recipe, it is done the same way. Using the same example of the recipe that yields 4 servings, if you required enough food for 8 people, divide 8 (required number of servings) by 4 (number of servings given in the recipe) and get a multiplier of 2. Multiply each ingredient by 2 to give you the correct amounts to adjust the recipe to yield 8 portions.

Although these examples may seem overly simple, this is the method to use to convert any recipe.

TEMPERATURE CONVERSION

Most often, we see temperatures given in terms of Fahrenheit. But, more and more we are seeing it listed as centigrade. In the event that it is listed one way, but, for your purposes, you would like to know its equivalency in the other unit of measure, do not despair. Listed are the simple formulas from converting from Fahrenheit to centigrade and from centigrade to Fahrenheit:

To go from Fahrenheit to centigrade, subtract 32 degrees and multiply the remainder by $\frac{5}{9}$ or .555. Example: 185 degrees Fahrenheit equals 85 degrees centigrade. $(185 - 32) \times .555 = 84.91$ or 85 degrees centigrade.

To go from centigrade to Fahrenheit, multiply the centigrade number by $\frac{9}{5}$ or 1.8 and add 32 degrees. Example: 50 degrees centigrade equals 122 degrees Fahrenheit. $(50 \times 1.8) + 32 = 122$ degrees Fahrenheit.

"COOKIN'"

Next time you're having fun in your kitchen, chop to the beat of our song called "Cookin'." This is the first full-length rap written by "The Clever Cleaver Brothers."

Sing along ......

We're "The Clever Cleavers" and we're here to say
We get into food in an intimate way.
Now don't get us wrong cause we really don't mean
To give you the impression that we're talking obscene.
It's just that food is our livelihood,
We know how to cook, others wish they could.

Now that you know just who we are,
Pull up a chair and don't go too far.
You'll tell your friends for miles and miles
About "The Clever Cleaver Brothers" zany style.
With meat to cut and veggies to clean,
We're waving our knives, you can see what we mean.
But when everything is said and done,
You can bet your bunch of parsley you're sure to have fun.

Steve Cassarino, that's who I am,
With pots and pans I really jam.
See, I move like gears with plenty of oil,
I heat up like a pot that's about to boil.
I like to eat, I like to have fun,
Let's put the two together, they should equal one.

Lee Gerovitz is the name you want to know.
And cooking with the ladies is the only way to go.
With a pinch of humor and a dash of flair,
The other TV chefs don't begin to compare.
I work the kitchen with obvious ease,
I dress in a manner that's sure to please.
Now The Frugal Gourmet might have had his day
But "The Clever Cleaver Brothers" are here to stay.

Remember friends, until we see you again, have fun cooking, because cooking is fun!

 We're sorry to say that we have to go,
It's been fun but it's the end of our show.
So with fork in hand and an empty plate,
Join us again with a smile on your face.

 Now don't despair, don't be sad or cry,
Listen to me and I'll tell you why.
It should be clear and easy to see,
"Cookin' With The Cleavers" is the place to be.

 Tell your friends you've seen the light,
"The Clever Cleaver Brothers" are one heck of a sight.
We cook, we dance, we'll even sing you a song,
Watch our show, you won't go wrong.

 Now grab some food and a pan or two,
It's your turn, see what you can do.
The meal was great, the dishes are done,
"Cookin' With The Cleavers" sure has been fun!

"OUR GUARANTEE"

"The Clever Cleaver Brothers" guarantee that you will derive some pleasure and/or satisfaction from this recipe scrapbook.

This book will put some unique dishes on the table, and *should* help to put some romance back in the candlelight dinner—and might even give you a laugh or two.

Lee & Steve
"The Clever Cleaver Brothers"

BIBLIOGRAPHY

Culinary Institute of America. *The Professional Chef.* 4th ed. Boston: CBI Publishing. 1974.

Day, Bunny. *Catch'em Hook'em & Cook'em.* New York: Gramercy Publishing. 1961.

"Forget About Cholesterol?" in *Consumer Reports,* March 1990.

Grundy, Scott, and Mary Winston, eds. *The American Heart Association Low-Fat, Low-Cholesterol Cookbook.* New York: Times Books. 1989.

Lundberg, Donald E., and Lendal H. Kotschevar. *Understanding Cooking.* Amherst: Univ. of Massachusetts. 1968.

Montagné, Prosper. *The New Larousse Gastronomique.* New York: Crown.

Scott, Jack Denton. "The Tree of Life," in *Reader's Digest.* Article on olive oil.

Shimizu, Holly H. "Do Yourself a Flavor." *FDA Consumer,* April 1984.

Witty, Elizabeth, "Cooking Oils – Separating the Good from the Bad," in *Price Club Journal* (San Diego ed.), February 1989.

Putting on our best face.

INDEX

A

B

C

O

Oil, cooking, about, 196–97; olive oil, 197
Omelet Loaves, Cheese, 40
Omelet, Steve's, 42
Onion Soup, French, 32
Orange
  Butter, 129
  Crepe Batter, 173
  Crown, Assorted Fruit in, 20

P

Pan Gravy (for Turkey), 135
Parmesan and Sausage Bread, 54
Parsley Rap Potatoes, 157
Pasta, 140–53
  Fettuccine Alfredo with Sun-Dried Tomatoes and Basil, 140–41
  Fettuccine Noodles, Seasoned, 83
  Lasagna, Baked, 150–52
  Linguine with White Clam Sauce, 142–43
  with Mussels in Marinara Sauce, 144–46
  Ravioli, Hot, with Pesto Sauce, 148–49
Pea Pods, Chinese, Sautéed, 170
Peas, Fresh, with Bacon, 166
Pepper Sole, 85
Pepperoni and Mozzarella Bread, 52

Pepperoni and Sausage Calzone, 64
Pesto Sauce, 148
Pilaf, Rice, 160
Pizza, 56–72
  Clever Cleaver Treasure Chest, 71
  Clever Seafood Calzone, 68
  Italian Delight, 60
  Italian Meatball Calzone, 62
  Pepperoni and Sausage Calzone, 64
  Vegetarian, 58
  Vegetarian Calzone, 66
  "White," 56
Pizziola Meatballs, Clever, 96
Pork, 102–13
  Chops, Stuffed Center, with Apple Butter, 106–7
  Ham, Baked Fresh, 105
  Loin, Roast, 103
  Ribs, BBQ by the Bay, 112–13; BBQ Sauce, 112; Honey Mustard Glaze, 113
  Stir-Fry, Tropical, 108–9; Curried Rice for, 110
  Tenderloin, Medallions of, 102
Potato(es)
  Baked, 163
  and Leek Soup, 30
  Parsley Rap, 157
  Roasted Quartered, 156
  Roasted Tournéed, 118
  Tournéed, 158
Poultry, 126–37. *See also* Chicken; Duck; Turkey about, 128
Puffed Apple Jacks, 40

CLEVER CLEAVER PRODUCTS

Cookin' With The Cleavers – $12.95 ($3.00 S&H)

If your book store is out of this unique cookbook, ask the manager to order you a copy. As an alternative, you can receive a copy(s) from Clever Cleaver Productions.

"Cooking For Compliments" – $19.95 ($3.00 S&H)

Beginner cooks, rejoice! This 60-minute video cookbook, covering 11 complete meals and a garnish scene, has been produced for you. The video employs our light-hearted, step-by-step approach and covers breakfast, lunch and dinner. "Cooking For Compliments" comes with an accompanying recipe booklet.

"The Cholesterol Zone" – $19.95 ($3.00 S&H)

This 35-minute videotape follows "The Clever Cleaver Brothers" as they decode the mystery, myths and facts about cholesterol with their light-hearted, educational style. The tape features simple low-cholesterol cooking alternatives, recipes, facts on saturated fats and oils, what to look for on packaged food labels, and general cooking tips. "The Cholesterol Zone" comes with a recipe booklet containing twenty-four healthful recipes.

Clever Cleaver Fan Club Apron – $11.95 ($2.50 S&H)

This durable Cookin' With The Cleavers apron holds up wash after wash. Whether you are at the store or behind the barbecue you will look like a pro. The "Official Fan Club" logo really sizzles.

- When ordering these products from Clever Cleaver Productions, California residents should include the appropriate sales tax.

To order these products or to write to "The Clever Cleaver Brothers" send your correspondence to:

Clever Cleaver Productions
968 Emerald Street
Suite 51
San Diego, CA 92109